Egg Money

A Tribute to Saskatchewan Pioneer Women

A Project of the
Saskatoon German Days Committee

ALICE MELNYK PUBLIC LIBRARY
Box 460, TWO HILLS, AB., T0B 4K0
Phone 657-3553

Copyright ©2012 Saskatoon German Days Committee

All rights reserved. No part of this work may be reproduced or transmitted in any form or by any means – graphic, electronic or mechanic, including photocopying, recording, taping or information storage and retrieval systems – without the prior written permission of the publisher, or in the case of photocopying or other reprographic copying, a licence from Access Copyright, the Canadian Copyright Licensing Agency. For an Access Copyright licence, visit www.accesscopyright.ca or call toll-free 1-800-893-5777.

Library and Archives Canada Cataloguing in Publication

Egg money : a tribute to Saskatchewan pioneer women / [edited by Deana Driver].

"A project of the Saskatoon German Days committee".
ISBN 978-0-9879643-0-4

1. Women pioneers--Saskatchewan--Biography. 2. Frontier and pioneer life--Saskatchewan. I. Driver, Deana, 1956-

FC3505.E55 2012   971.24'020922   C2012-901370-6

Editorial Committee – Barbara Hoggard-Lulay (Chair), Brigitte Boldt-Leppin, Rosa Gebhardt and Barbara Stehwien
Editing and book design – Deana Driver, Al Driver
Cover photos – Deana Driver
Inside photos courtesy of – Saskatoon German Days Committee, the 24 pioneer women's families, John Penner, Deana Driver
Maps & map compilation – B.Stehwien, P.Geo., Saskatoon, SK, February 2012
Sources: Geological Atlas of Saskatchewan, general Internet research and family archives of the pioneer women

Printed and bound in Canada.

DriverWorks Ink
110 McCarthy Blvd. N., Regina, Saskatchewan, Canada S4R 6A4
www.driverworks.ca   (306) 545-5293

CONTENTS

FOREWORD	7
INTRODUCTION	11
STORY OF THE SCULPTURE	15
MARTHA BLOMQUIST (1865-1935)	26
THERESA MARIA KLUHSPIES (1878-1952)	32
ANNA MARIA GEBHARDT (1878-1979)	38
ELIZABETH SCHINOLD (1882-1971)	44
OLIVE WULLUM (1882-1970)	50
JOSEPHINE STONE CROWLEY (1884-1972)	54
ANNA KATARINA HOLMSTRÖM TEGSTRÖM (1888-1971)	60
ELLEN CARLSON STRINHOLM (1889-1951)	66
THERESIA LEIBLE (1889-1968)	78
CECILIA KIEFER (1892-1978)	84
JULIA KUNKEL (1892-1968)	90
MARIE L. FLEUTER (1893-1976)	96
MABEL PETTY KERR (1895-1981)	104
SADIE MCDONALD (1896-1971)	110
EDA STRINHOLM MALMGREN JOHNSON (1897-1985)	116
ROSALIA REMAI (1898-1971)	122
JULIA SAJTOS (1903-1971)	128

Matilda Jabusch Wudrick (1905-1987) 132
Rosa Durand (1906-1997) 136
Mary Dyck (1912-1980) 142
Lena M. Kloppenburg (1915-1968) 148
Bertha Riekman (1915-2004) 154
Helen Goertzen Wiens (1917-2000) 160
Margaret Ezak (1923-2011) 168
Acknowledgements 175

Foreword

Experiences throughout my life have led me to contemplate forces that converge to place one at a certain point in time, influence choices, and steer the direction of life's journey. Given that we live in a world that is exceedingly fast-paced, ever-changing, fiercely competitive, yet dangerously fragile, it is easy to forget that we are not the first or the only generation to face uncertainty and angst.

There are important lessons to be learned from stories such as those featured in this impressive volume. Each is an important reminder that, as Canadians, we are truly fortunate citizens. The privileges that we are afforded are a mere dream to many people living elsewhere in the world. The advantages and conveniences that we take for granted could not have been imagined by preceding generations.

It is impossible to fully grasp the challenges faced by the wives, mothers, grandmothers, sisters, and daughters whose accounts are shared on the following pages. Story after story involves adversity, heartbreak, isolation, and loss. Yet, common threads of faith, love, determination, optimism, and generosity weave through each narrative. The chapters depict innovators and entrepreneurs, caregivers and multi-taskers to the extreme. They laboured from early morning to long into the night, selflessly tending to the needs of home and family.

These were outstanding individuals, indeed. Their stories and those of other pioneer women have, traditionally, been absent from the pages of our history books. Therefore, a volume such as this can be considered a treasure for the information and details that it preserves. In addition to being a valuable resource, *Egg Money* is truly engaging and uplifting.

The Canada that we know and appreciate today would certainly be a different place, were it not for bold, resilient, and incredibly hard-working women. We are blessed citizens to have inherited tremendous legacies. The challenge now is to create new legacies for the benefit of generations to come.

The Egg Money sculpture and this precious collection of stories are both significant steps in bringing long-overdue public profile to the roles played by women in the unfolding of our beloved province and nation.

– The Honourable Lynda Haverstock
 C.M., S.O.M., Ph.D., LL.D.

Introduction

In the late 1800s, the region now known as Canada's Prairie provinces was a vast unpopulated area of plains and forest with settlements of mostly First Nations and Metis people dotting the landscape. In a desire to add more residents to this largely unexplored wilderness, the Canadian government enacted legislation to entice settlers from Europe and other parts of North America to venture into the unknown and make a new life for themselves in this 'promised land'.

The *Dominion Lands Act* of 1872, based on the *Homestead Act* of 1862 in the United States, allowed settlers to acquire one quarter of a square mile of land in Western Canada to homestead for a small $10 registration fee. These 'free' homesteads of 160 acres (64.75 hectares) were offered to settlers who cultivated 10 acres annually and built a residence within three years of a registered intent to settle a specific land claim.[1] The settlers had no overall control over the land, as it remained a property of the Dominion until 1930 when it was transferred to the provinces. This initial offering of property had the desired effect, however. Although slower than the Canadian government had wanted, the Prairie provinces saw a marked increase in population.

About 170,000 people settled in the three North-West Territories between 1881 and 1886. During the first three decades of the 20th century, Saskatchewan was Canada's fastest growing province: between 1900 and 1930, there were 303,000 homestead entries. The population grew from 91,000

---

[1] *The Encyclopedia of Saskatchewan, Dominion Lands Act,* Elizabeth Mooney

in 1901 to 932,000 in 1936, and the number of farms increased during this time from 13,000 to 142,391.[2]

Between 1900 and 1910, the British were the largest immigrant group arriving in Canada (562,054), although the numbers of Americans (497,249) and, to a lesser extent, continental Europeans (394,088) increased dramatically at the end of that decade. While many of the British were attracted to the developing industrial heartland of Ontario and Quebec, Americans and continental Europeans were more responsive to the opportunities presented by settlement in the West. Between 1897 and 1910, 32% of arrivals from continental Europe and 42% of arrivals from the United States made homestead entry in Western Canada. This influx of population and the development of an economy based primarily on agriculture played a direct role in the creation of Saskatchewan as a province in 1905.[3]

Unstable political regimes and economic hardships in their homelands were the main reason that Europeans were prompted to make the arduous journey to Saskatchewan in the 1800s and 1900s in search of a better life. European farmers had very little hope of owning land or securing a future for themselves and their families. The promise of a new start in what was believed to be a free, fertile land across the ocean beckoned them. Honest tales of hardship coming from relatives who had already settled in Western Canada were not enough to deter many from leaving their homelands and reaching for their dream. Men and women braved the elements and dangers of a new land, sometimes with their children in tow.

German-born Julianne (known as Julia) Kusch was the first European woman to settle in Saskatoon, Saskatchewan. Born in 1839 in the city now known as Gdansk, Poland, Julia came to Canada with her German-born husband Karl in the 1860s. They lived in Ontario and then farmed in Manitoba. In April 1883, Julia and Karl arrived in Moose Jaw by railway and set off with their seven children (ages two to 16) and other Temperance colonists on the 150-mile trek north to Saskatoon. On that month-long journey, the Kusch family braved a spring

---

[2] *The Encyclopedia of Saskatchewan, Farming,* M. Rose Olfert
[3] *Encyclopedia of Saskatchewan, Geography of Saskatchewan,* Randy Widdis, quoting Minister of the Interior, *Immigration Facts and Figures* (Ottawa: King's Printer, 1910)

snowstorm and other adventures including their ox-drawn covered wagon getting stuck in muddy water along the trail.[4]

Julia was the only woman in this wagon train of settlers and she was taken aback by the scene that greeted them in Saskatoon. In a 1917 article in the *Saskatoon Daily Star*, Julia said land agents lied to entice the family to move to the settlement. They were told there would be a store where they could buy supplies, but none existed.

"The 'picturesque bend in the South Saskatchewan River' was lost on my great grandmother," says Frank Kusch. "Emerging from the wagon, she looked about the tiny settlement of a few lone bachelors, some sod shacks and tents and asked, 'Where's the town?' Someone pointed to a stand of poplars. 'Three crows sat in the trees,' Julia mused later. 'And that was Saskatoon.'" Karl had to travel back to Moose Jaw to buy supplies the family needed, leaving his wife and children with the other colonists during his 15-day trip.

Julia was pregnant when she arrived in Saskatoon and her eighth child, Henry, was born in November 1883. Henry Kusch is said to be the first white baby born in Saskatoon and the Kusch family is known as the first family of Saskatoon. Their homestead was near the present site of the University of Saskatchewan.

"The Kusch family's first home was a pitched tent, then a sod hut and by the following summer a stone house, serving as both a family dwelling and a shelter for their animals (along with the settlement's first cat)," says great grandson Frank Kusch. "They felled trees and floated logs down the river to fashion the first buildings. Work was unending, but quitting was not an option for pioneers. They overcame numerous hardships as they built the first homes, stores, schools, churches and committed the first of their brethren to the ground (all the while sidestepping a rebellion and some 'hostile' Indians)."

In that 1917 newspaper article, Julia commented on those difficult early years in Saskatoon. "We lived in terror," she said. "Every time the dog barked at night, we thought the Indians were coming. We watched for them day and night."

---

[4] *The Sword of Saint Paul*, D.F. Robertson

Nonetheless, the Kusch family prospered and acquired significant tracts of land in the growing town over the next quarter century. They were best known for donating the land that is the site of St. Paul's Cathedral on the banks of the South Saskatchewan River.

Julia Kusch's story is similar to those of so many other pioneer women who struggled to make a home in a harsh new land. With limited supplies and often relying on only inner strength, these women stood alongside their partners or braved the challenges on their own to help create a strong, proud foundation for the province of Saskatchewan.

This book honours the stories of some of those courageous pioneer women.

Story of the Sculpture

In 2005, Saskatchewan's centennial year, a small group of men and women of German heritage met in Saskatoon to plan a German Days celebration to be held later that year. For various reasons, including the shunning of Germans after the First World War, this was to be the first such celebration since 1932, when the last Saskatoon German Days was held.

After discussing numerous ideas for the celebration, it was decided that the theme should be 'Share our Story'. A suggestion was made by Rosa Gebhardt to honour German pioneer women of Saskatchewan. Many of the members of this German Days Committee commented that these 'unsung heroes' in the province's history were deserving of more recognition for their work in helping to build the province. The suggestion to honour these women was adopted unanimously.

The Saskatoon German Days' centennial 'Share our Story' project was held October 1 and 2, 2005, in front of Saskatoon City Hall. Special guest speaker Margaret Dutli, former professor of St. Thomas More College, presented a tribute to pioneer women. She cited their work as life-giving and life-sustaining in face of isolation, loneliness and hardship.

"They came from several parts of Europe. Some were looking for a new life. Some were forced to leave their homes because of oppression and persecution," said Dutli. "They were a faith-filled, hopeful people: Mennonite, Hutterite, Baptist, Catholic and Lutheran. They came with their customs, their culture and their dreams."

Dutli noted that the men were enticed by the promise of free land and wonderful opportunities, "but did they have any awareness of what they were asking of the women? Mosquitoes, black flies, grasshoppers, bedbugs, head lice, prairie fires, drought, dust storms, frost, hail, prairie winters, bone-chilling cold, blizzards with no trees for shelter. They felt prejudice because they were Germans, because they did not speak English, because they had large families, and because their customs were different."

Dutli spoke of the unending labour involved in baking, churning, growing a huge garden, canning and preserving, raising chickens for eggs and for meat, but also of the beauty they created through flower gardens, houseplants, embroidery and lacework. Quilting bees helped stave off isolation and loneliness, as did their regular gatherings for worship, dancing or visiting.

"They learned of the wild fruits and herbs from their Aboriginal neighbours – saskatoons, chokecherries, gooseberries, strawberries and medicinal roots and herbs. Some of the women served as nurses and midwives. Others took younger ones under their wings, comforted and encouraged them. In spite of the forces against them, they guarded and passed on their rich customs and culture, and their folk wisdom. Today, in our centennial year, it is fitting that we show our gratitude to the German pioneer women for their brave and resourceful legacy in building the mosaic that is Saskatchewan."

Leading up to the German Days celebration, Gebhardt had stated that these pioneer women deserved more than mere words of tribute during the celebration. "I said, 'Words are not enough. Could we do a sculpture or something more permanent to honour them?'"

This idea was enthusiastically supported and at the German Days event, it was announced that a permanent statue would be sought to honour pioneer women of Saskatchewan. At the wrap-up meeting after German Days in October 2005, Gebhardt and Sabine Doebel-Atchison were delegated to search for a sculpture. At first, the idea was hatched to hold a contest to create the statue, but that proved overwhelmingly complicated and prohibitive in time, energy and finances, so they decided to search on the Internet to see if an appropriate sculpture could be found.

They discovered photographs of a bronze sculpture created by Shirley and Don Begg of Studio West Bronze Foundry in Cochrane, Alberta. The sculpture, appropriately named 'Egg Money', consisted of a larger than life-size woman feeding chickens, a girl and boy holding chickens and eggs. It was perfect for their project.

They immediately contacted Studio West and learned the artists were looking for a placement for their third and final bronze statue before they intended to destroy the mould. Two similar sculptures had already been placed in Cochrane and Fish Creek, Alberta. In April 2006, the Beggs were contracted by the Saskatoon German Days Committee to reserve the 'Egg Money' sculpture.

Shirley Begg was particularly delighted to have been approached about this use of their sculpture, in keeping with her grandmother's idea for the creation of the statues. "My mother's mother, Mabel Cargo, was a really remarkable woman. She was a bride, a widow and a mother in just about a calendar year. Her husband died in an accident just before my mother was born. She was an entrepreneur. She took the insurance money and bought a grocery store, then a lumber mill, then built onto her farmhouse. Into her 100s, she still balanced her own chequebook," says Shirley Begg.

"She spoke of the hard lives of the women who were her customers in her country store in Water Valley in Alberta. They took on so many burdens. She said many of the women who came into her store worked beyond their strength."

Shirley was having tea with her 102-year-old grandmother when the statues of the Famous Five women were in the news, honouring the women who caused a 1929 court to declare women as persons under the *British North American Act*. Begg's grandmother was concerned that ordinary pioneer women were being forgotten. Even their names were forgotten since the family names were those of their husbands.

"She said, 'You know, somebody should make a statue of an ordinary Prairie farm woman.' She looked across the table and said, 'You make statues. Hand me my chequebook. Let's start a fund.'"

Mabel Cargo also instructed her family to ask for donations to the fund instead of flowers for her own funeral. "She died a few weeks short of 106."

Shirley admits feeling a special thrill when she was contacted about the statue by the Saskatoon German Days committee. "I was very excited because when we did the first of the three, I really wanted all three to be in the Canadian Prairies. That's what my grandmother and I really wanted to honour." The first statue is at The Ranche in Fish Creek Provincial Park in Calgary and includes the woman, two children and the chickens. The second one is located at Centennial Plaza on the main street of Cochrane and honours the 100th anniversary of the town. That statue includes the pioneer woman, chickens and a cream can. The Saskatoon statue has all four elements to it.

"Egg money in some families was known as 'Mother's money' and the title was symbolic of the many ways that women earned their income," says Shirley. "On the Prairies, if you sent a poem into the weekly paper and they published it, sometimes that money was what paid the taxes if they didn't have a good crop. The egg money is what brought the telephone in to some farms."

After contacting the Beggs, the German Days statue committee began two years of work creating public awareness and requesting assistance for the project. To finance the sculpture, a donation of $1,500 was requested from families wanting to have the name of their mother or grandmother permanently engraved around the base of the sculpture. Although the German Days Committee initiated the project, the members were adamant that all nationalities be invited to have their pioneer women represented.

The committee approached the City of Saskatoon for a suitable location for the sculpture. They asked if it could be erected in the new River Landing development along the

South Saskatchewan River to commemorate the area where the earliest immigrants landed. In their application, the committee stated: "We envision the sculpture for Saskatchewan pioneer women to become a social space where Saskatonians will want to meet and remember the contributions their ancestors of only a few generations ago made to the province."

On June 23, 2008, almost three years after the German Days 'Share Our Story' celebration, Saskatoon City Council approved and announced the location for the bronze sculpture 'Egg Money' at the corner of Avenue B and Sonnenschein Way, near the new Saskatoon Farmers' Market. A *Saskatoon StarPhoenix* article about the project highlighted the goal of raising more than $100,000 for the sculpture. This generated many positive responses. Families of several pioneer women

Mabel Cargo, celebrating her 102nd birthday, with her granddaughter Shirley Begg of Studio West Foundry

expressed interest in participating. Ellen Remai of the Frank & Ellen Remai Foundation approached the committee, offering major sponsorship of the project. This was an important and exciting step, bringing the dream of a sculpture closer to reality. With this commitment from the Remai Foundation, the committee entered the final phase of the project.

The foundry received the go-ahead to cast the sculpture, a technical consultant was hired to be the liaison between foundry and city, and thoughts turned to the unveiling process. In fittingly pioneer tradition, the Mennonite Central Committee (MCC) quilting group Piecemakers for Peace was asked to craft a king-size quilt in log cabin design to cover the life-size statue prior to the unveiling. About 400 hours of work went into creating the stunningly beautiful quilt. The committee later donated the quilt back to the Mennonite group and it was auctioned off at the MCC's annual relief sale in June 2010.

Studio West Foundry is one of the very few foundries that does every step from beginning to end – from creation of the design to installation. The task of erecting the beautiful Egg Money statue took about three days as the individual pieces took shape to create this striking monument honouring pioneer women.

Plaques interspersed in the base of the sculpture carry the names of 24 pioneer women specifically recognized by their family's contributions to the project. These women came from various corners of the province and many nationalities including American, British, French, German, Hungarian, Norwegian, Russian, Scottish, Swedish and Ukrainian. Sponsors, especially the Frank and Ellen Remai Foundation, were also permanently recognized in the sculpture.

The Egg Money statue's main inscription states:

"Pioneer life on the Prairies was not easy. Women, assisted by their children, raised chickens and sold eggs to buy essential items for their families. The resourcefulness of these women helped families and communities survive during the pioneer times from the late 1800s onward. The German community of Saskatoon, in a spirit of gratitude, honours

Saskatchewan's pioneer women from all ethnic backgrounds, for lives of courage, hardship and perseverance. This monument serves to commemorate them."

In the late 1920s, Saskatchewan farm women sold eggs for about three cents a dozen to buy essentials or, in some cases, extras for their families. One Saskatchewan woman recalls as a child being sent into town by her mother to sell a dozen eggs for three cents and purchasing a one-cent stamp to mail a letter to family in Ontario. Anyone purchasing eggs from a store in those days paid about 36 cents a dozen.

At the unveiling of the Egg Money statue in Saskatoon on the afternoon of September 20, 2009, Ellen Remai commented on her own family's heritage. "I feel extremely lucky to have been given the opportunity to sponsor this meaningful and loving tribute to the pioneer women who gave so much and asked for so little in return. When I first heard of the Egg Money sculpture, I thought, 'What a great idea. What a wonderful way to honour and celebrate the pioneer women of Saskatchewan!' I knew instantly that I wanted to be part of this project.

"This project holds a special place in my heart. Both my mother, Rosa Durand, and my mother-in-law, Rosalia Remai, were proud, courageous pioneer women for whom I have the greatest respect and admiration. They, too, collected eggs and sold cream for a little extra money to care for their large families. These heroic women were truly remarkable. They faced incredible obstacles. But, with their strong spirits and inner strength, they found ways to overcome their daily hardships. The Egg Money sculpture, created by Don and Shirley Begg, is a timeless, loving tribute to these courageous women who made a lasting imprint in our province. They are my heroes!"

Above left: A multicultural dance was part of the Saskatoon German Days celebration, October 2005
Above right: Studio West artist Don Begg with a marquette of the statue

Above and below: The statue installation begins in downtown Saskatoon in the new River Landing development along the South Saskatchewan River, a spot commemorating the landing of the earliest immigrants

Above: Sabine Doebel-Atchison (left) and Rosa Gebhardt with a miniature of the 'Egg Money' statue
Below: Granite plaques honouring contributors to the project are ready to install

Story of the Sculpture

Above and left: The sculpture installation took three days

Above left: The base is prepared for one of the chickens
Above right: The Mennonite Central Committee's quilting group created a log-cabin design quilt to cover the statue prior to the unveiling
Below: The statue, as it stands today

The Egg Money statue honours Prairie pioneer women of all nationalities

Below left: The cream can's inscription recognizes the Frank & Ellen Remai Foundation's contributions to the project
Below right: The plaque celebrates the courage and resourcefulness of Saskatchewan's pioneer women

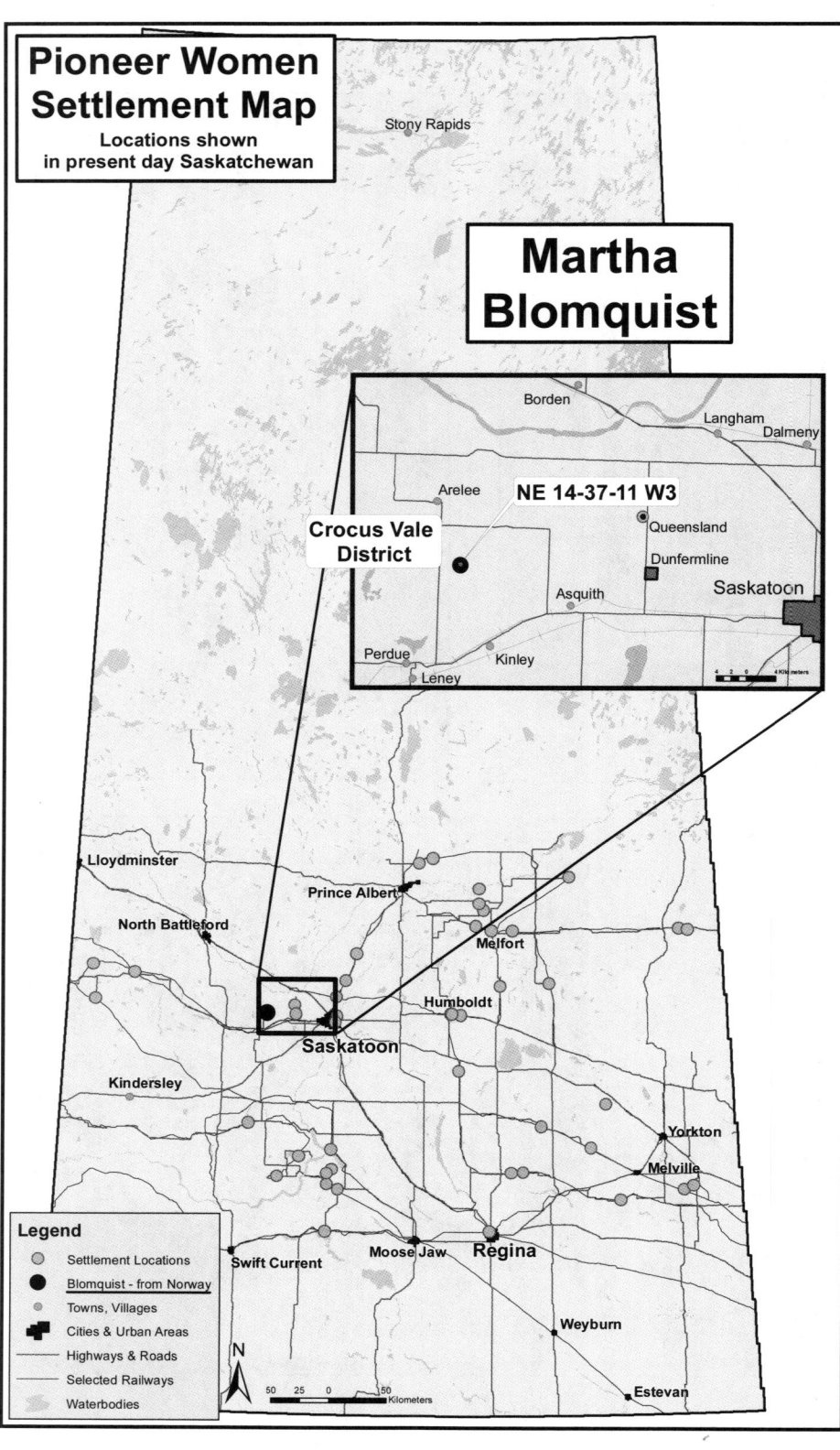

Martha Blomquist
(1865-1935)

Marthe (Martha) Johannesdatter Bjelde and her twin sister Kari Johannesdatter Bjelde were born on the Bjelde farm in Aurland, Norway on June 14, 1865, to Johannes Knutsen and Marthe Olsdatter. Marthe and Kari were the seventh and eighth children in the Bjelde family. The family lived in the Sogn Og Fjordane fylke (municipality) in the Parish of Urland and the farm was called Bjelde med Skaar. Marthe and Kari were baptized June 25, 1865, and confirmed June 13, 1880, in the local parish Vangen Hoved (now known as Aurland).

On February 28, 1887, at the age of 21, Marthe Bjelde boarded a Stjerne Line ship from the port of Bergen to begin her emigration to the U.S.A. In Norway, Martha was spelled Marthe. After arriving in the United States, her first name was always spelled Martha.

On November 14, 1888, Martha married Guttorm Monson Ohnstad in the Nora Lutheran Church near Gardner, North Dakota. Guttorm's family had arrived in the U.S.A. in 1874 but the Bjelde and Ohnstad families knew each other when they were in Norway. Guttorm and Martha farmed beside the Red River, raised cattle and owned and operated a butcher shop in Perley, Minnesota for many years.

Martha and Guttorm had five children: Mons (1889), Marie (Mary) (1890), twins Johannes and Karen (Carrie) (1892), and Gilbert (1894). Johannes lived for only a month or so after his birth.

In the winter of 1894, a fire broke out in the town of Perley and Guttorm helped carry water from the Red River to fight

**John and Martha Blomquist on their
wedding day, November 1896**

the fire. He developed pneumonia and died on February 9, 1894, at the age of 36. He is buried beside his parents and many family members in the Nora Lutheran Church Cemetery. Gilbert was born a few months after his father's untimely death.

Widowed with three young children and a fourth child on the way, Martha now had to manage the farm and business. Lukris Bjelde, one of Martha's sisters, arrived from Norway to help. John Blomquist, a farmer from nearby Grandin, North Dakota was hired to manage the farm. John and Martha soon fell in love and were married November 14, 1896, in Fargo, North Dakota. John Blomquist was born in 1864 in Narke, Sweden and had come to North Dakota in 1888 to work as a farmer. Martha and John's daughter Hilda was born in 1898.

In the fall of 1902, Minnesota and North Dakota farmers received news of homestead land being available in Saskatchewan, Canada. This intrigued John Blomquist and his friend Carl Halvorson. They immediately headed north and a few days later, arrived in Saskatoon and filed on land for themselves and by proxy for at least a dozen other Minnesota and North Dakota families. This land was about 40 miles west of Saskatoon in the Crocus Vale district.

John went back to North Dakota for the winter and returned to Saskatchewan in the spring of 1903. By June, he had brought Martha and the five children to Saskatchewan. Their first home was 20 feet by 24 feet in size and cost $700 to build. It was located in the Rural Municipality of Eagle Creek, North-West Territories. Martha gave birth to two more children, Clarence (1907) and Arthur (1912).

The Blomquists arrived in Saskatchewan with a bit more than most settlers had, due to John's astute business mind and the proceeds from the Ohnstad farm. They brought 11 horses, 10 cattle, machinery plus household and personal possessions. The Blomquists kept a supply of kerosene, flour and various staples on hand, which were made available to other settlers. The Blomquist home was a place of welcome to all and many people made it a stopover on long treks.

In 1908, the railroad was extended from Saskatoon to an area south of Asquith. Hauling grain several miles with horses was a long tiring process, so having a shorter distance to deliver grain was a tremendous help for the settlers.

War broke out in 1914, which caused grain and other prices to soar. For the next 10 years, most farmers prospered, acquiring more land, horses and cattle. Many built new homes, barns and other buildings. In 1917, the Blomquists built a large T. Eaton-style two-storey house and a new barn. The buildings were equipped with electricity generated by their own plant.

In 1918, the Spanish influenza swept through the region. Many homes were struck and devastated by the deaths of family members. The Blomquist family was no exception as their eldest son Mons died at the age of 29.

Martha was one of the original members of the Crocus Vale Ladies Aid, which was formed in the early 1920s. Most of these women were from Scandinavian countries. Their get-togethers had the dual purpose of being a social time as well as being productive. The ladies made quilts, raised funds for worthy causes such as the Red Cross, assisted the church and, later on, packed boxes with items such as candy, cookies and other treats as well as hand-knit socks, handkerchiefs, reading materials and cigarettes for soldiers who were overseas fighting in the Second World War. They took turns hosting the Ladies Aid gatherings each month and everyone contributed food to the lunch afterwards. Crocus Vale Ladies Aid functioned for almost 55 years.

Martha had a reputation of being a very kind, generous person. As an adult, Martha often walked across a field to the neighbouring farm carrying a pail of milk for the Wilcox children since they did not have a milk cow at that time. The Wilcox family used to say, "If there was an angel on earth, it was Martha Blomquist."

Martha was small in stature but had a big heart. When going to visit a neighbour, she always took "a little something" along, such as preserves or baking. The coffee pot was always on in Martha's kitchen and coffee was usually served with cookies.

Since John had acquired extensive holdings of land and ran two threshing crews, this required hiring many men and also a few young, local women to help Martha in the kitchen. The Blomquists treated their hired help like family. John was known as an honest, fair man to work for and Martha saw that they were all well fed.

Edna Cowley, one of the young hired women, married Clarence Blomquist in December 1928. After the wedding, John and Martha graciously offered their home for the wedding dance. This was a surprise since Martha did not approve of dancing, due to her strong Lutheran faith. Edna often commented on how wonderful it was of her new mother-in-law to allow dancing in her home in honour of their marriage.

Martha passed away on September 7, 1935. The memorial gates at the Crocus Vale Cemetery were erected by John in 1936 in memory of Martha and son Mons. John passed away December 27, 1941.

By Audrey Rawlyk, granddaughter (daughter of Clarence)

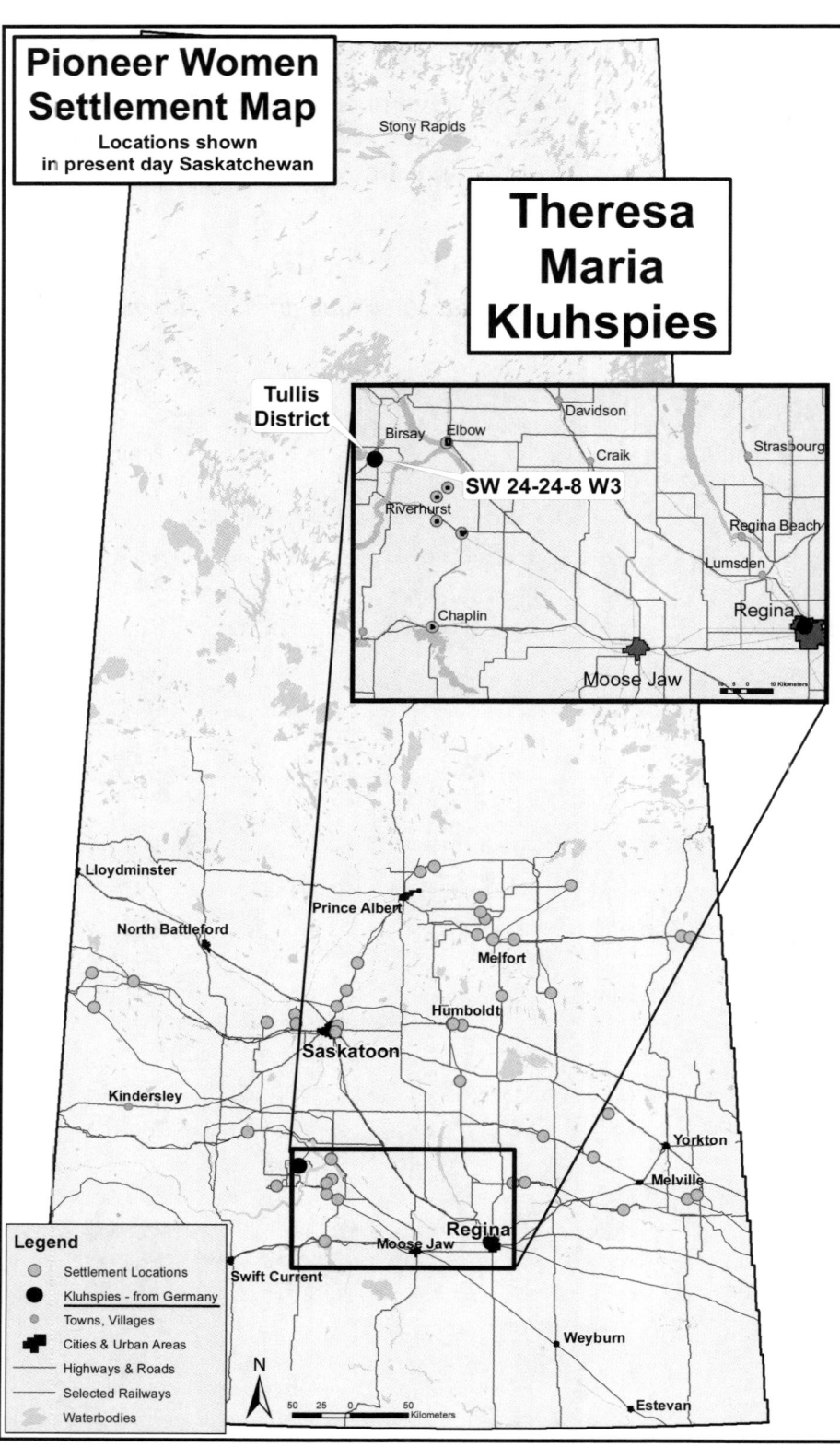

THERESA MARIA KLUHSPIES
(1878-1952)

Theresa was the third child born to Michael and Maria (Bornberg) Holl in Würzburg, Bavaria, Germany, on September 22, 1878. She was the only girl in the family with five brothers – Michael Jr., Joseph, Valentin, Ignaz, and Cuthbert. As a young girl, Theresa went to school and later worked in the vineyards.

She left Germany in 1903 for the United States and worked in New York for five years as a nanny for a German Jewish family. While in New York, she attended St. Patrick's Cathedral for Sunday Mass.

In 1907, she moved to Regina, Saskatchewan to reconnect with Phillip George Kluhspies, whom she had previously met in Germany. They were married on June 9, 1908, at St. Mary's Roman Catholic Church. Phillip had left his homeland in 1901 and worked in the United States for three years before immigrating to Canada. In June 1905, he filed his papers for his homestead in an area known as the Tullis District.

After Theresa and Phillip married, they made the journey from Regina to Phillip's homestead near the hamlet of Tullisville, four miles south of Birsay, Saskatchewan. Homestead life was very lonely for Theresa after city life, but Phillip had built a two-room lumber house for them, which was more comfortable than the sod houses of many other settlers. Their home was often the halfway stop for pioneers travelling from the Beechy area to Davidson. Many people stopped in for a meal and a bed for the night. The couple had

**Theresa Kluhspies around 1903
and in 1940 (insert bottom right)**

many tough years but were able to keep livestock of a cow or two, a few pigs, chickens, ducks and geese, along with horses to help with the farm work.

A good neighbour to those in the community, Theresa was often called to be midwife or to help families during times of sickness. The coffee was continually on and a sandwich or a piece of cake was offered to anyone who stopped in for a visit or to ask for some help.

In the early days, Theresa and Phillip travelled by horse and buggy or sleigh. They bought their first car in 1927. It was a Pontiac with an Indian on the hood.

The Kluhspies were blessed with the birth of two daughters: Katherine Anne (1909) and Maria Theresa (Daisy) (1910). Daisy had infantile paralysis at about the age of three, which left her with disabilities. Theresa always said that Daisy was her cross to bear. Daisy became her commitment for the rest of Theresa's life.

Katherine attended Hanford School in the home district and later Sion Academy in Moose Jaw and school in Saskatoon. She married James King in July 1938. They gave Phillip and Theresa six grandchildren: Joan, Harold, Lorne, Yvonne, Neil and Wayne.

Theresa grew a big garden every year and enjoyed planting a variety of items that were slightly extraordinary for her location. Her grandchildren remember asking questions about kohlrabi, broad beans, snow peas and the various herbs and spices their grandmother carefully tended.

Theresa and Phillip retired from the farm in 1946 and moved into the town of Birsay. Katherine and James then moved to the farm. During the summer months, Theresa occasionally served dinner for the family on Sundays after church. She always made lemon pie from scratch, so the entire family eagerly looked forward to dessert.

Theresa spoke broken English with a German accent, but spoke German whenever she had the opportunity. In harsh winter months, the grandchildren sometimes stayed in Birsay with their grandparents during the week so they would not miss school. This was a special time when the children could have "dunka" – coffee with lots of milk in it – and could dunk their slices of homemade bread into the cup and eat the soggy bread. They were told not to tell their mother because she did not approve of this practice. Katherine thought the children should eat their bread properly and then drink from their cups.

Theresa was a typical frugal pioneer woman. When her grandchildren were visiting, she insisted that they choose only one item to have on their bread – either butter, peanut butter or jam. She always said, "When we own two houses, you can have two things!"

Theresa was a loving person who taught some of her grandchildren how to sew and knit. She made many dresses for the granddaughters, and knit many socks and mitts for all of the children. She learned to accept the hard life of a pioneer woman and was always cheerful and glad to see company at the door.

Theresa passed away on October 24, 1952. She is buried in Woodlawn Cemetery in Saskatoon beside Phillip, who passed away on March 20, 1953. After Theresa's death, their daughter Daisy was moved to a home in Weyburn and later to Moose Jaw for care. Daisy passed away April 25, 1965.

By Joan Scott, granddaughter (daughter of Katherine)

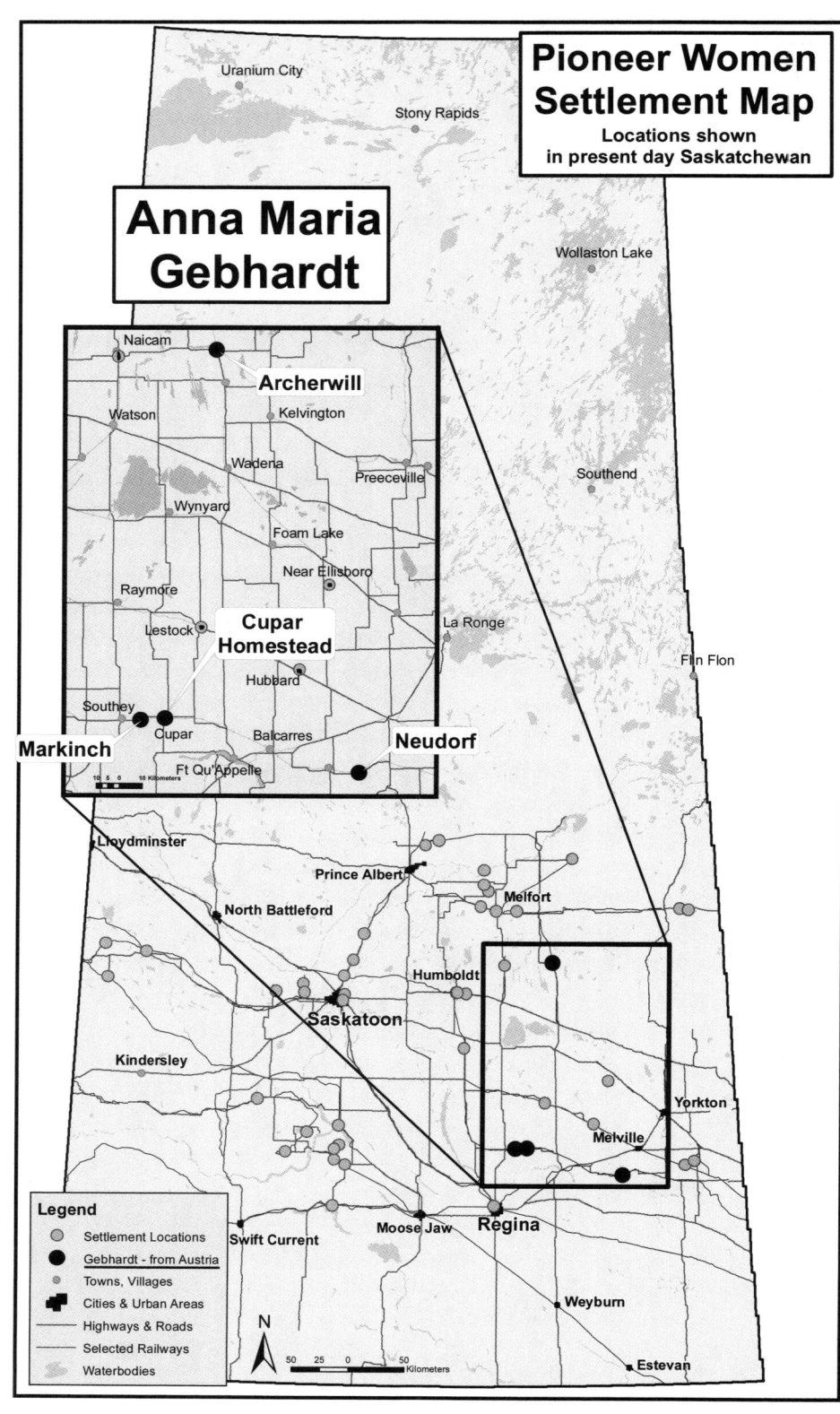

ANNA MARIA GEBHARDT
(1878-1979)

Anna Maria was born on November 29, 1878, in Galicia, former Habsburg Empire. The forefathers of Anna Maria and her husband Johann Gebhardt migrated with many fellow German Lutherans from Alsace-Lorraine, Rhineland, Baden-Württemberg and Switzerland in the latter half of the 1700s to form new colonies in Russia. Empress Catherine II (1762-69), after steadily expanding the Russian Empire into western and southern territories, wished to quickly settle these new areas with skilled agriculturalists who were loyal to her. The Empress, also known as Catherine the Great (Princess von Anhalt-Zerbst married Tsar Peter III), extended an invitation to farmers in Germany to establish ethnic colonies in Russia. Her proclamation promised free land, a farmhouse, freedom of religion, military exemption and no taxation for 10 years. Hence, many thousands of farmers were lured to southern Russia, northwest of the Black Sea, forming new villages, of which many were purely German.

The first Gebhardt shown in the parish records was Georg Gebhardt, born on April 17, 1775, in Ugartsthal, Galicia. He was the great grandfather of Johann Gebhardt. Later, the Gebhardt family and others moved on to the town of Scholtoi in Bessarabia which had been annexed from the Ottoman Turks in 1812.

Anna Maria married Johann (John) Gebhardt on May 1, 1894, and they made their home in a small village (Dorf) in Scholtoi. Anna Maria never talked much about the earlier

**Anna Maria and Johann Gebhardt on their
60th wedding anniversary in 1953**

years but said they had an orchard, a garden and enjoyed a river (Fluss) flowing nearby. They ate apples, pears and plums and raised cows, geese, chickens and pigs. Meat was not plentiful due to the lack of refrigeration. Many meals were called Mehlspeise[5].

The progressive erosion of rights and privileges granted by the Empress – especially those of military service, cultural and linguistic freedoms – caused Germans to emigrate from their colonies in the late 1800s. Again, it was the lure of inexpensive farmland that made several Scholtoi families consider the long and arduous trip to Canada. Johann's older brother Phillip and family left Russia in 1903 to settle in Melville, Saskatchewan.

In 1906, 28-year-old Anna Maria embarked on the same journey with her husband Johann and their four small

---

[5] Meatless meals based on flour

children: Adolf (12 years), Carolina (seven years), Wilhelm (three years) and baby Eleanor, who died en route at the age of eight months. They arrived in Saskatchewan after about five months of travel. In the village of Neudorf, Anna Maria and her family spent the first winter in a wagon box turned upside down since there was no time to build a sod house.

In 1907, Johann filed for a homestead north of Cupar. In 1910, the couple had a 16-foot by 30-foot log house valued at $300, a stable, one granary, a 14-foot by 20-foot storehouse valued at $300 and 10 acres of fenced pasture. Between 1908 and 1919, six more children were born. Anna Maria gave birth to 13 children in total. Heinrich, Valentin, Eleanor and Emma died in infancy. The nine who lived to adulthood were: Adolf, Carolina, Wilhelm, Philipina, Philip, Elisa, Wilhelmina, Rudolf and Maria.

They lived a simple life, speaking mainly German since most of the settlers in the district shared the same background and Lutheran faith. They homesteaded in the Cupar area and worked the land with oxen and later with horses. In 1919, they moved south of Markinch, where Johann built a two-storey house along with a larger barn and animal shelter.

The Dirty Thirties struck and the family had to lie on the floor many times with wet towels across their faces waiting for the wind, loaded with topsoil and sand, to die down. Nothing grew during those years, except for Russian thistles and tumbleweed that rolled up against the fences. Sand and drift dirt piled up so high that only the tops of the fence posts could be seen. It was a very bad time.

During the drought years, the government offered 160 acres for $10 in what was considered northern Saskatchewan. So Johann and Anna Maria, Wilhelm, Rudolf and Maria moved to Archerwill, where there was a good water supply and, most importantly, rain. Philip, Elisa and Wilhelmina stayed in Markinch. By that time, Adolf, Carolina and Philipina were living on their own.

In the Archerwill area, they built a log cabin and animal shelter. The family planted and harvested in order to also keep the Markinch home supplied. With the abundance of practical knowledge that Johann and Maria had, the family was able to live off the land and slowly recover from the early 1930s. And finally the rains came back. Johann and Anna Maria along with Philipina, Rudolf and Maria moved back to the Markinch farm in 1936. Wilhelm and Wilhelmina stayed in Archerwill.

In 1940, Johann and Anna Maria retired to a small home in the town of Markinch and took life easier. They enjoyed their home and small garden and learned how to relax. They always had time for friends and family, which they richly deserved.

After Johann died in 1962 at the age of 90, Anna Maria lived with family until 1965 when she moved into the Lutheran Home in Regina. She still knitted and crocheted at the age of 95 but her sight and hearing slowly dimmed from then on. Her mind however, remained alert and she enjoyed visits from family and friends.

Anna Maria lived for 100 years and died in February 1979. Anna Maria is buried next to Johann in the peaceful Wheatwyn Church Cemetery, which is a designated provincial heritage site.

Anna Maria's life exemplified the pioneering spirit. Endurance, hard work and determination moved her family forward often in most difficult and challenging times. Anna Maria was a caring woman and had a strong faith in God. Her whole life was centred on God, the church and her family. Her motto was, "You do your best. God will do the rest!"

By Mary Schneider, daughter

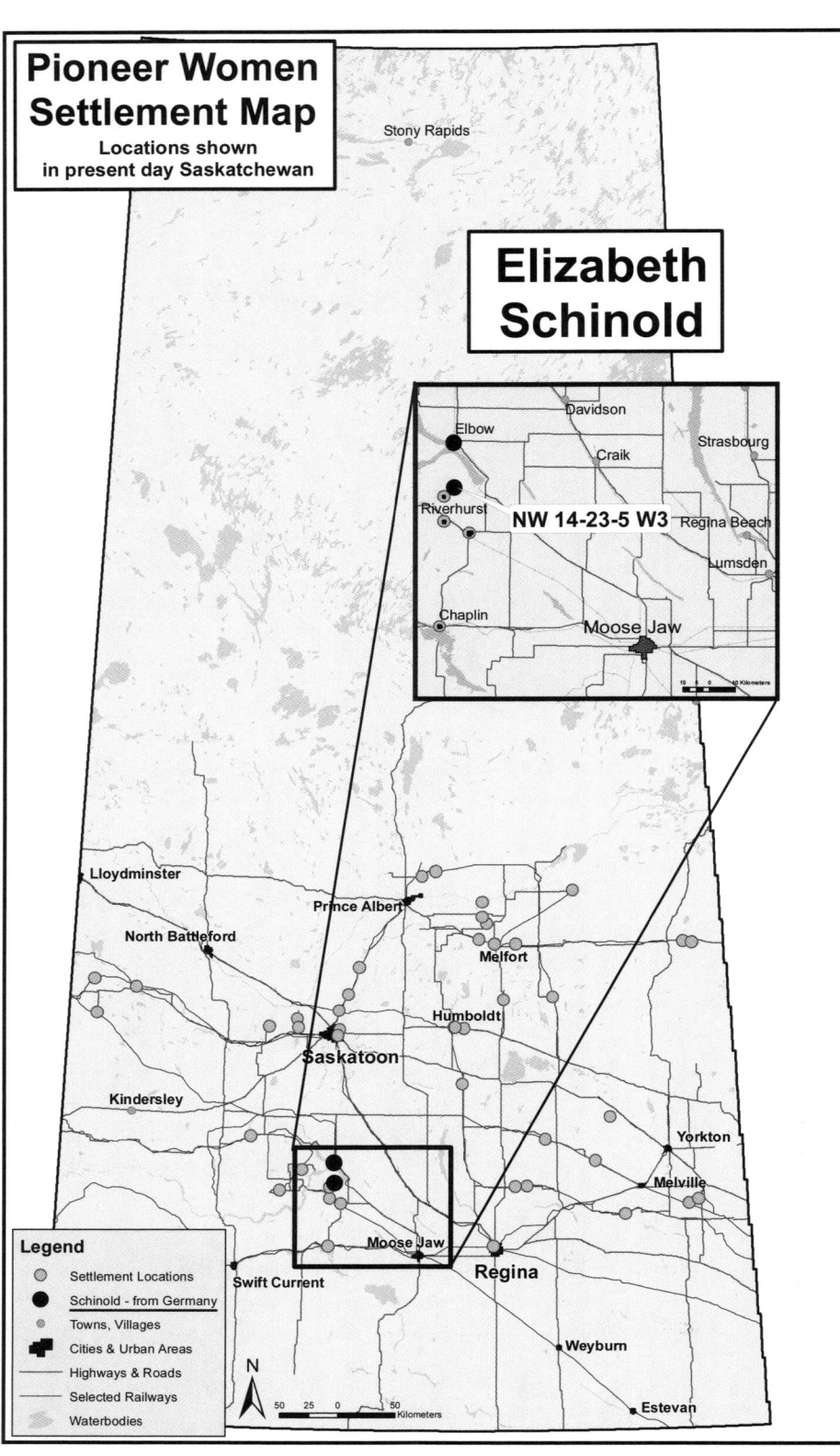

Elizabeth Schinold
(1882-1971)

Born Elizabeth Blanche Bichel, Elizabeth Schinold was christened Elizabeth but called Lizzie throughout most of her life. She was also known as "Grandma the Great" in later life – a title that still endures.

Lizzie was born on November 19, 1882, to Christina and Peter Bichel on a farm in Strawberry County, not far from Salina, Kansas. She was the ninth of 10 children, two of whom died in infancy, and was only 12 years old when her mother died following surgery on the kitchen table. Little is known about Lizzie's mother, who came to the U.S.A. from Germany at age two with her widowed mother. More is known about Lizzie's father, also an immigrant from Germany and a civil war veteran. He was industrious and had a well laid-out farm in Kansas with water piped into the house from a spring, and a dumbwaiter[6] in the kitchen. Lizzie often spoke of the family's orchards, of drying apples and making apple cider and sauerkraut.

On September 26, 1906, Lizzie married George Ignatius Schinold, a young man who farmed nearby. The newlyweds moved with George's brother Joe to Elbow, Saskatchewan the following spring because of the promise of land there. They travelled by railway but could afford only one freight car. At one end of the freight car, they put a wagon box on its side to serve as their living quarters for a month. Their freight car also held four horses, a cow, a walking plough, a rake, the rest of the wagon, a blacksmith outfit (bellows and an anvil), all their

---

[6] A lift on ropes and pulleys which is dropped to the basement to keep food cool and then raised back to the kitchen

Lizzie and George Schinold with their children: (left to right) Grace, Verona, Joseph, Lauretta, Wendel, Margaret, Georganna and Irene

household effects, a dog named Shep, a barrel of water and another barrel of dried apples. Only one person was permitted to ride for free, so during the many stops the train made, two of them had to hide in the wagon box. When they arrived in Saskatchewan in May, Lizzie was pregnant and they had 35 cents with which to start their new life.

On the trek by wagon from Davidson to Elbow, Lizzie went snow blind and recuperated for several days at the Larmer farm before moving on to their homestead. This was their introduction to Canadian hospitality.

Once they reached their homestead, they lived in a tent while building their sod house. The house was upgraded when windows were added and it proved very comfortable. It was heated with buffalo chips and stayed warm in the winter but cool in the summer. However, the roof leaked when it rained and continued to do so for days after the rain. Mice were also a problem, but it was home until some years later when they built a house. George was also inventive and the house included a well that brought water from the basement and a dumbwaiter in the kitchen.

In August 1907, Lizzie gave birth at home to her first child, Irene, who was followed by Georganna, Margaret, Lauretta, Wendel, Joseph, Verona and Grace (1920).

Lizzie's life on the farm consisted of raising her eight children, feeding the chickens, milking the cows, making butter, bread and soap, and washing clothes on a washboard. She also made the majority of the family's clothing, cutting her patterns from newspapers. She always planted a huge garden, and rhubarb was a standby that was added to everything. In berry season, she took the children to the nearby sandhills for a day of berry picking. They brought home 100-pound flour bags full of saskatoon berries, raspberries and chokecherries. In the fall, Lizzie and the older children stooked the grain after George cut it with the binder. Every day during threshing season, Lizzie prepared three very large meals for the threshing crew, as well as substantial morning and afternoon lunches that were taken out to the fields.

Lizzie was very creative and could feed a crowd at a moment's notice. The coffee pot was always on and nobody was turned away from the dinner table. Often, the huge dining room table had to be set twice to feed everyone. She frequently sent pies and fresh loaves of bread home with visiting bachelors.

The farm prospered in the early years, and George built an impressive barn in the 1920s to mark their accomplishments and faith in the future. Then the Great Depression came with its drought and grasshopper infestations. Years later, their sons Wendel and Joseph often told a story about a farmer who left his harnessed team of horses standing while he went into the house. When he came back, the grasshoppers had eaten the horses and were playing horseshoes to see who got the harness!

Stories and songs lightened the mood for the family, but life was very difficult. The government gave the farmers bran, molasses and poison to mix and spread over the crops, but it wasn't enough to kill all the grasshoppers. Many of George and Lizzie's neighbours left their farms. George and Lizzie were told by others that they should leave as well, but they were determined to stick it out. Like other farm wives, Lizzie found even more ways to "make do." One of the most creative came when they couldn't afford a Christmas tree. Lizzie found a huge round Russian thistle that was bleached a silvery white. Once decorated, it was lovely.

When first-born Irene wanted to attend high school, George's first response was that there was no money. But Irene dreamed of being a teacher and George and Lizzie somehow found the money to enable her to live with her grandparents in Elbow through her high school years and then advance to Normal School[7]. Later, they supported a second daughter to become a teacher and another to become a nurse.

Tragedy struck when Irene became ill just as she started her teaching career. Her parents sent her to the Mayo Clinic but nothing could be done. She coped for 20 years with what is now thought to have been Multiple Sclerosis or Parkinson's disease, before succumbing at the age of 40. For most of those 20 years, Lizzie and the other children took care of Irene in their home until hospitalization was necessary. Even then, the nuns were impressed with Lizzie's diligence and they intervened when George faced his final illness and hospital beds were scarce.

Lizzie's story is much like that of other pioneer women. What stands out for her descendents is not just what she did, but how she did it. She was her husband's partner in the family farm and they together demonstrated values such as hard work, honesty and compassion and regularly attended Sunday mass at the Catholic Church in Elbow. While raising their family, they also gave to the community. George was a school trustee, the local teacher boarded at their house and Lizzie was a member of the women's church group. They were highly regarded by their neighbours and gave generously but quietly to those in need.

As a woman, Lizzie was strong without being strident. She worked hard but regarded hard work as "good for you" and was ever cheerful, warm and welcoming. She had a zest for

---

[7] A school to educate teachers

life and loved people. In her older years, she loved to travel but refused to fly because it left no time to talk to passengers. She wanted her children to have a better life. She gave them that and more. She left a legacy that lives on and inspires the generations that have followed.

Lizzie and George moved to a home in Moose Jaw for a time after retirement but Lizzie returned to the farm permanently after George died. She remained there until her death in 1971. Lizzie Schinold is buried at Elbow Cemetery, as are many other members of the Schinold family.

By Elizabeth's daughter Verona Evenson, and Elizabeth's granddaughters Carol Harvey (daughter of Grace King) and Pam Churchill (daughter of Lauretta Bowers)

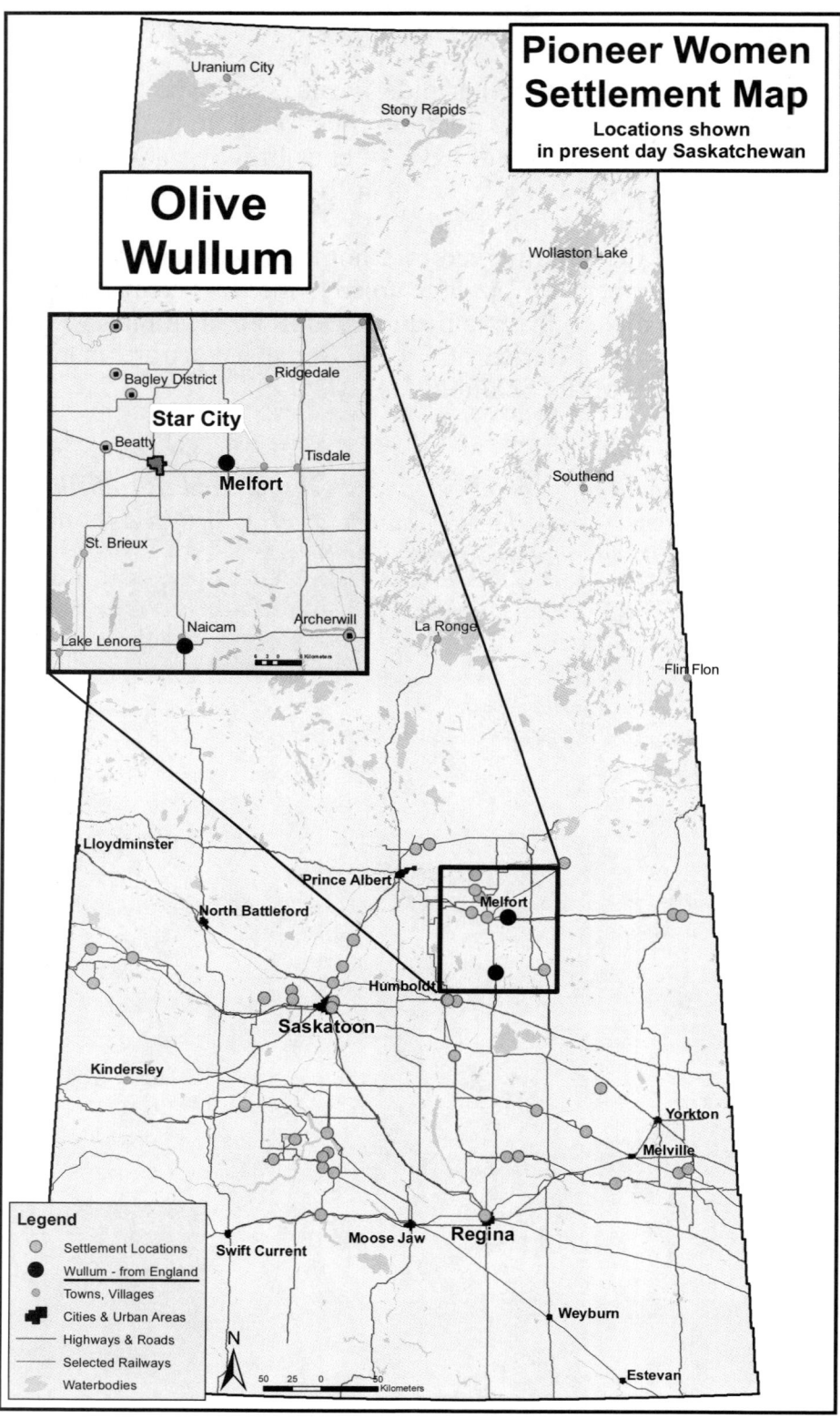

Olive Wullum
(1882-1970)

Olive Hounslow was born in New Headington, Oxford County, England on December 13, 1882. As a young woman faced with limited prospects at home, she decided to set out for North America, arriving in North Dakota to live with her aunt, Bessie Sculthorpe. There, at the age of 24, she met and married John Wullum, a Norwegian immigrant 19 years her senior, and together they relocated from North Dakota to the small Saskatchewan community of Star City, north of Naicam in the Melfort area.

In this district, the two newcomers raised eight children: Lovisa Ann (1906), Carl Edward, Nellie Charlotte, Albert Arthur, May Olive, Thelma Anna, John, and Lewis Emil (1924). Supporting a family of this size while also attempting to 'prove up'[8] a homestead posed considerable challenges for a couple thrust into unfamiliar surroundings with little prior agricultural experience.

Their eldest child was the first infant of European ancestry in the Star City district and when resources proved scarce, they relied upon the skills of Aboriginal neighbours to supply the growing family with fresh meat. On one memorable occasion, Olive heard what she thought was one of the local dogs scratching at her front door, eager for one of her cookie treats. Upon looking out the window to greet it, she instead found herself face to face with a black bear. Startled but undaunted, she scared the critter off but an impression remained: merry England had been left far behind.

---

[8] Cultivate 10 acres annually and build a residence within three years

Olive and John Wullum

In September 1910, John filed for a homestead south of Star City in the Lac Vert area and the family moved there. The mail was only delivered once a week and family members had to walk about a mile into the village to get mail or groceries. Since they were halfway between Watson and Melfort, the family had lots of visitors as people stopped in on their way to or from either town.

A number of different missionaries came through the area and the Wullum children were baptized either Anglican, Lutheran or Methodist. Olive taught Sunday School by mail for many years.

While life on the Parkland homestead had its moments of excitement, adjusting to its relative isolation and the monotony of farm and household chores was not easy. As one of her daughters recalled, "Mama was always singing, because besides being a naturally happy person, it helped to ward off the loneliness, which must have been dreadful at times in the early years." Not one to throw up her hands in despair, Olive applied herself to learning the skills that were crucial to the family's material well-being: she learned to milk a cow and churn butter, gardened, and ground barley by hand in a coffee grinder to make her own bread. The loaves may have contained a few husks, but the taste never suffered.

Like many other pioneer women, she also raised chickens and sold the eggs for four cents a dozen (and yes, they were 'free-range'!). In addition to the daily work of the farm, she also made sure there was occasionally time for fun, including singsongs, dancing and picnics. The family enjoyed picnics in the summertime at Lac Vert and during the winter, they often had evenings filled with music, as some of the neighbours played violins, mandolins and mouth organs. In her later years, she did a lot of knitting and she loved her flower garden.

After the passing of her husband in 1952, Olive moved to a small house in Naicam and remained an active member of the Anglican Church Women. She passed away in the town of Watson in 1970. She is buried in the Pleasantdale cemetery beside her husband John.

By Jenny Kerber, great-granddaughter (granddaughter of Louise)

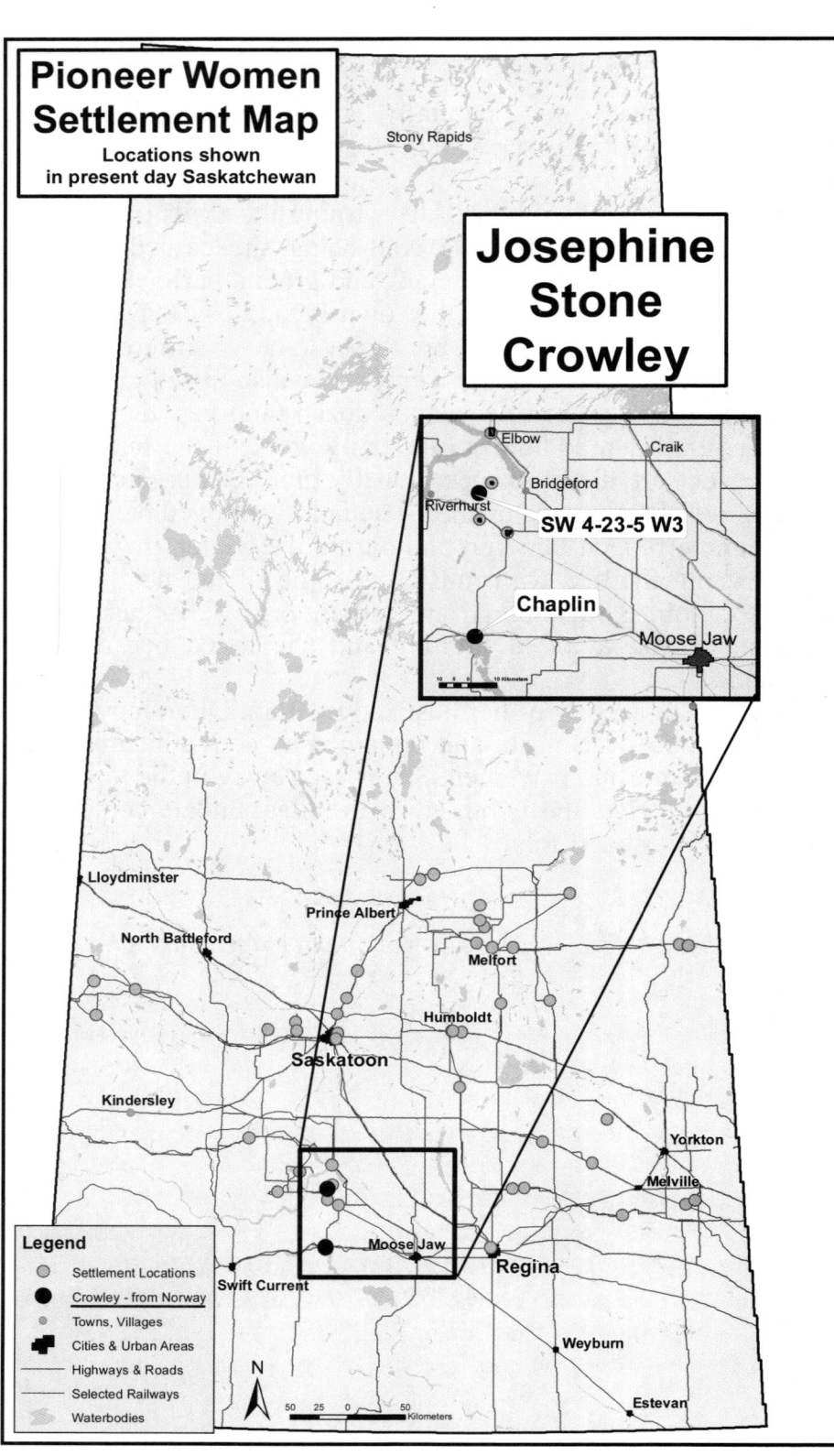

JOSEPHINE STONE CROWLEY
(1884-1972)

Josephine was born on December 1, 1884, above the Arctic Circle on the banks of a fjord in Sagely, Balsf, Tromso Co, Norway. She was the fourth child of Pauline Jacobsdatter and Hans Andersen. On December 26, 1884, she was christened Josefine Hansine Hansdatter in the church at Tennes. Her older siblings were Anna, Soren and Nils.

In 1887, her father Hans decided to immigrate to the Americas to improve the family's fortunes. Hans felt that as a blacksmith, he could earn a good living for the family. He had also farmed in Norway so thought the move was a good idea.

The voyage was like many others at that time, with all their worldly goods loaded onto carts to get them to the ships. After landing in Quebec City, the family travelled by train to the plains of the United States. They were informed upon entering the United States that there were too many Andersens, so their last name was changed to Stone. Some of their first names were also changed. Josefine became anglicized to Josephine (known as Josie), Anna became Annie and Soren became Julius. Nils stayed Nils.

In North Dakota, they found a settlement of Norwegians. They proceeded to set up a new home in a new country with their new names. Tragedy struck in 1888 when Josie's father suddenly died. Her mother Pauline was left alone in a strange land, unable to speak English, with four children under age 12. Fortunately, everyone in the family was already used to hard work from their life in Norway and they coped as a family unit. Her brothers worked for other settlers, her sister Anna

Josephine and Jack Crowley

did hired-girl work and four-year-old Josie helped her mother with the chickens and cows.

At the age of nine, Josie went to work in a hotel in Vang, North Dakota, so she could attend school there. Josie learned to read and write English but had to leave school after Grade 4 and work full time.

By 1900, all the good land had been taken in North Dakota and Minnesota, where her brothers Julius and Nils had both worked. The family decided to go north to Canada and get the 'free' 160 acres of land the Canadian government was offering to settlers.

They had to work and save to buy livestock and equipment, but the children were now old enough to do so and they all thought this would be a good new adventure. Their mother Pauline was also ready to pioneer again.

Josie's mother and brothers first travelled to the North-West Territories about 50 miles northwest across country from modern-day Chaplin, Saskatchewan to each get a homestead. They were in Saskatchewan when it became a province in 1905. Josie's sister Anna had met and married a grain buyer in Vang, North Dakota, so she stayed in Vang with her new husband. Josie stayed behind in Vang for several months with the rest of her family's belongings until the brothers could build a soddie[9] house in Saskatchewan to accommodate their possessions.

In the spring of 1906, Julius went back to Vang to get his sister Josie plus the rest of their livestock and the household effects. They travelled to Chaplin via an immigrant train which was crowded and had slat seats. They had to wait a week in Chaplin for the rest of their belongings to arrive. Brother Nils then met them with oxen and a wagon and on June 5, 1906, they were off to make the rest of the long trip to the homestead. Josie got her first taste of Saskatchewan weather during this trip when it snowed! Nils, Julius and Josie were wet and miserable and had to sleep on the ground under the wagons. At last, they arrived at the sod shack, where their mother was waiting and worrying.

In 1908, Josie returned to Vang, N.D. to help her sister, Anna Vinen, and Anna's family move to Saskatchewan. This time, the trip to the homestead was made in a horse-drawn rig. Pauline was happy that her four children were all now in the same vicinity. Anna and her husband later moved to nearby Bridgeford where he resumed his career as a grain buyer.

Josie did outside work on the farm, taking care of chickens, milking cows, haying and hauling wagonloads of grain to Bridgeford, a 30-mile distance. This freed up the men for breaking land. Many of the other pioneers did not have a farming background and were 'green' to the ways of the West. Josie found there was a good market to sell her family's garden produce, eggs, milk and cream to them. She also started baking bread for the bachelors in the district, some of whom were there getting their homestead ready on their own. The Stone family was used to the farm way of life but it was

---

[9] Term used by settlers as a reference to a sod-built house

difficult to get good water. Years later, there were deep wells dug in some places but it seemed impossible for the Stone family to get a well dug that actually produced potable water. They had to rely on a slough for their drinking water.

Josie loved gardening and grew a nice garden every year. She also brightened the sod shack with houseplants and they were in every home in which she lived. They were her joy.

The pioneers made their own fun with house parties, card games and dances. It was likely at one of these events that she met Jack Crowley, another homesteader who lived about seven miles east of Julius and Pauline's homestead. In 1912, Josie and Jack married and she moved to his homestead.

After marriage, Josie simply moved her workload to a new locale. She still did all the inside work and the same amount of outside work she had done before. Jack was a justice of the peace and in those days, he was kept busy. He was also a councillor for the Rural Municipality of Maple Bush and later reeve. This required him to be away a lot, leaving the running of the farm on Josie's shoulders.

Josie gave birth to Jessie May (1913), Annis Douglas (1915) and David John (1916). She often took her small children with her to do farm work. Josie always had at least seven milk cows and she'd place the smallest child in the manger so it would not get trampled by a cow while she did the milking. Cream cans filled with rich cream were shipped to the city of Moose Jaw. Eggs were sold locally. Garden produce was canned for winter use and there were berry-picking trips for saskatoons and chokecherries. There was no refrigeration, so beef and chickens were also canned. Pork was cured in brine in big crocks into ham and bacon. Nothing was ever wasted.

By the late summer of 1914, things were looking very good for Josie and her siblings. The crops were good and harvest was expected to be great. Nils and his wife were expecting their first child. Anna and her husband were settled and expecting their fourth child. Josie and Jack were doing well and expecting their second child. Julius was engaged to be married in 1915. The trouble in Europe seemed far away and they were all close together, as they had been in Norway.

In February 1915, Anna died following childbirth complications, leaving her husband with three small children and a new baby. A Bridgeford family took the baby to raise as their own. Anna's husband then died the following year, leaving the remaining three children orphans. These children went to live with their Aunt Josie and Uncle Jack.

Josie was a remarkable woman, raising her own small children (newborn to age three) along with eight-year-old Mary, six-year-old Helen and four-year-old James Vinen, and still doing all the inside and outside work as she had done before. In her spare time, she was busy knitting socks and mitts for the whole family.

She was a member of the Lawson Ladies Aid and the Prosperity Rebekah Lodge #81 until her death. She never complained about the hard work she had done. It was just how things were, and she made the best of it.

Josie suffered a stroke in 1970. She died in October 1972 after a lifetime of hard work. Josie is buried beside her husband Jack in the Riverhurst Cemetery.

By Mavis Birch Moore, granddaughter (daughter of Annis)

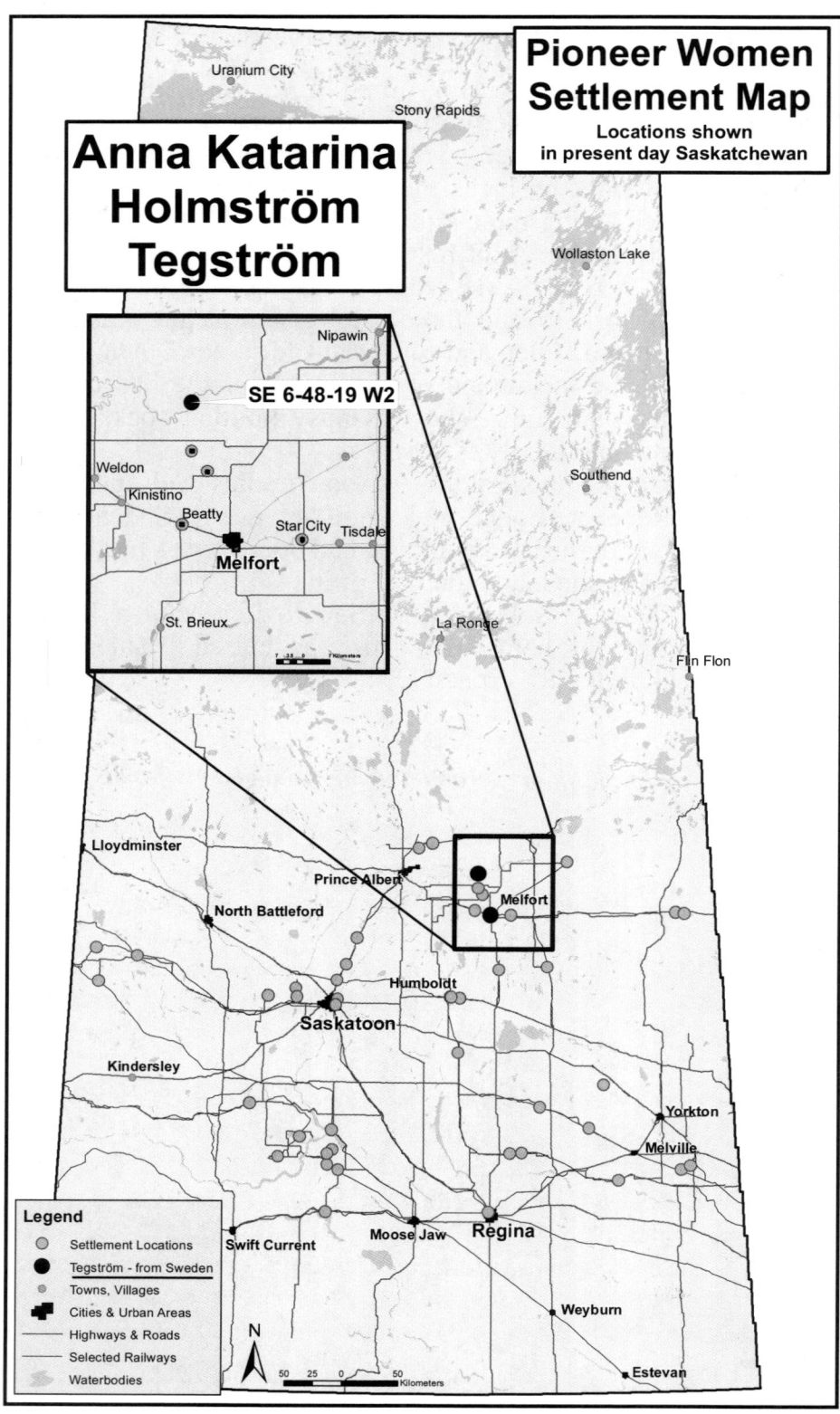

Anna Katarina Holmström Tegström (1888-1971)

Anna Katarina Holmström was born on May 28, 1888, in Finnäs, Våle, Jämtland, Sweden. As a young girl, she worked as a housekeeper and herded cattle in the valleys and mountains near the family's farm.

She married Nils August Tegström in Sweden in May 1910. Nils was born in Bjurholm, Västerbotten, Sweden in 1885 and immigrated to South Dakota in 1905 with his brother Olaf. Nils and Olaf worked for three years loading and unloading boats on the Missouri River and building roads and working on the railroad before Nils returned to Sweden in 1908.

Shortly after their marriage, Nils and Anna left Sweden for Canada and homesteaded about 20 miles northwest of Melfort. The homestead papers were signed on October 11, 1910. Timber was cut by axe to build a small house in May 1911. Axes were also used to remove trees and land was broken with horses. Anna and Nils never returned to Sweden and Anna never saw her parents, her sister Selma or her brothers Johan, Gustaf, Per, Nils and Axel again.

Anna and Nils had nine children: Agnes (1911), Melvin, Annie, Ole, Martha, Minnie, Alma, Alice and Ellen (1927). Nils spent most winters away from home hunting and fishing to provide for the family and logging for a new and bigger house.

Nils passed away in February 1932 at age 47 and Anna was left alone with young children. The eldest soon married and moved away from home. A new house was built in 1940,

Anna and Nils Tegström and daughter

mainly from the logs that Nils had cut during the winters. It was a 1½-storey home with a porch, kitchen, pantry, living room and two bedrooms on the ground floor. The upper level was used mainly for storage but there was also a finished bedroom. A small dirt cellar below the pantry was accessed through a trapdoor and stairs.

Anna's sons Melvin and Ole had married and were living reasonably close by, so they seeded and harvested the crops but Anna milked cows, raised chickens and cared for a big garden. A 'cream hauler' came by on a weekly basis to pick up cream cans and egg crates to be delivered to the Melfort Creamery. There were always plenty of canned meats, fruits and vegetables in the pantry and in the earthen cellar. An icehouse situated in the yard was used to keep certain perishables such as cream and butter from spoiling.

Anna always had tunn bröd (thin bread), fresh baked bread, cookies and pastries in her home. She was a very good cook and that ability was passed on to all her daughters. Somehow, she kept a 'starter'[10] over winter and in the summer, all the children were given a small amount to make their own tjock mjölk (thick milk), which was a yogurt-like product that poured from a pitcher very slowly, something like molasses in January! They used to have it on cereal or just as a treat in a dish with sugar sprinkled over it.

Anna's two eldest grandchildren, Wayne and Dale Malmgren, spent some weekends with their grandmother during the spring or fall. They walked the two miles from Pine Bluff School on Friday when school was out and stayed until Monday morning when they walked back to school. They were brought up speaking some Swedish at home, so were able to converse with their grandmother. They enjoyed their weekends with her and helped with milking cows, doing chores and weeding or hoeing in the garden. Dale remembers that she was hardworking and welcoming, very neat and tidy (both herself and her home) but that she must have been quite lonely. The boys often walked with their grandmother to spend a few hours visiting their Uncle Ole and his family half a mile away.

Another grandchild, Ken Tegström, was given the chore as a youngster of delivering wood by horse and caboose to his grandmother during the winter months. He unloaded the wood and was always invited in for a treat – usually a five-cent chocolate bar or cookies or cake. Anna would prata Svenska (chat in Swedish) to him. Ken couldn't speak Swedish so conversations were quite limited until he learned to understand over time and was able to chat with her. Anna never learned to speak English but was able to understand a little bit and say a few words. One of the younger grandchildren, Elaine, remembers her as, "The granny with the white hair, always in a bun, who always spoke Swedish – which I couldn't understand."

Anna lived alone on the farm until 1957, when she sold it and bought a small home in Melfort. She lived in that house

---

[10] A small amount of cultured product for use in warmer weather, to add to fresh whole milk to make the yogurt-like thick milk

until she became ill and was hospitalized. Anna's sense of humour remained with her until the end. Upon visiting her in December 1970, her grandson Dale asked in Swedish, "Vet du vem jag är mormor?" ("Do you know who I am, Grandmother?") Anna replied in Swedish, "Om du inte vet vem du är, hur kan du då tro att jag ska veta det!" ("If you don't know who you are, how do you expect me to know?")

Anna Katarina Holmström Tegström passed away on March 13, 1971.

By Dale Malmgren, grandson (son of Annie Tegström)

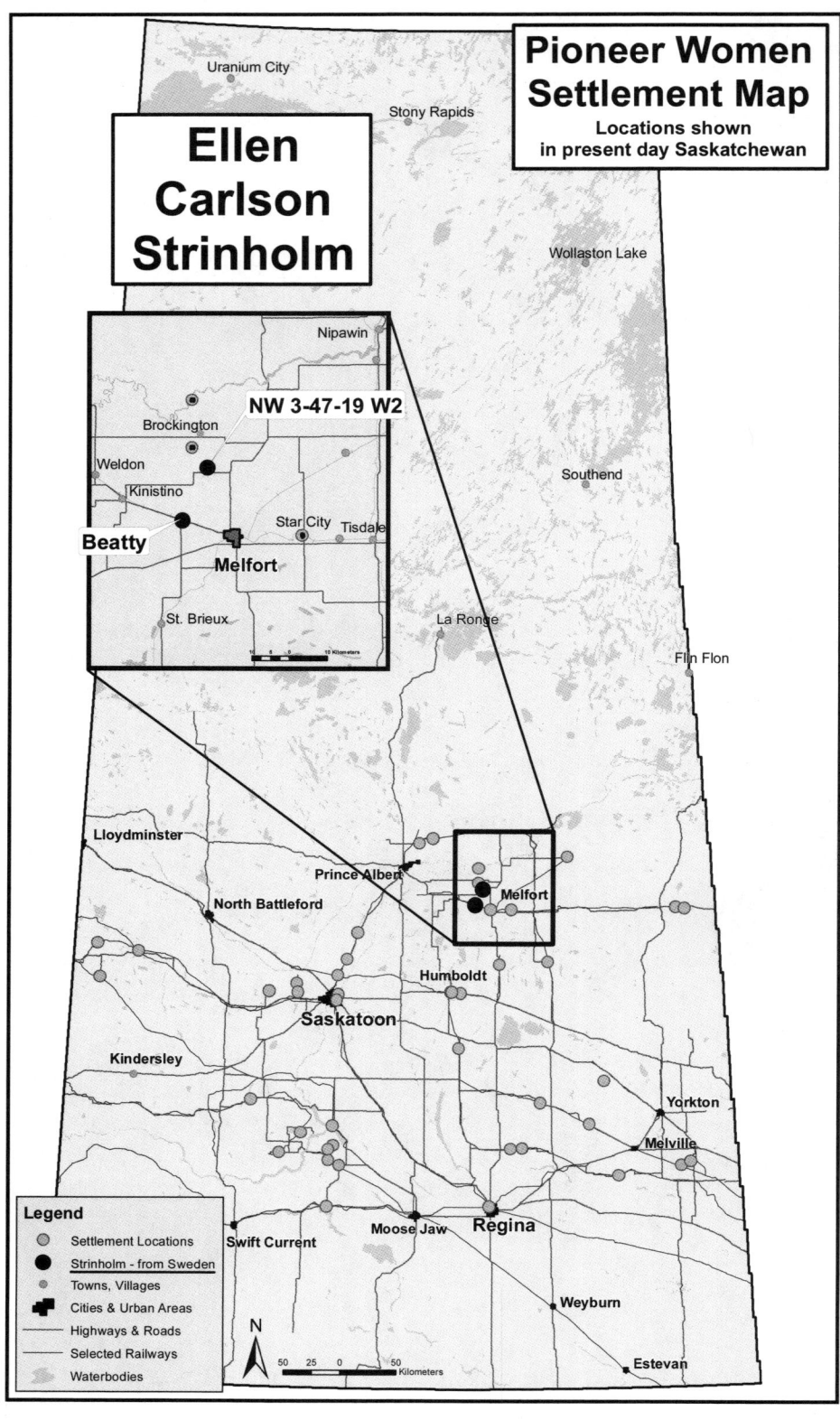

ELLEN CARLSON STRINHOLM
(1889-1951)

Elin Teresia Karlsson (Ellen) was born on July 19, 1889, in Skivsjon, North Degerfors, Vasterbotten, Sweden. Her father, Karl Eriksson, was a farmer well known for his singing. Her mother, Anna Lovisa (nee Jonsdotter), was a gifted baker whose puff pastries and other delicacies were in high demand for weddings in Sweden. Ellen's mother was a strong, independent woman known to have smoked a pipe with a curved stem. She stood firm for what she believed was best. When Ellen was eight years old, Anna Lovisa brought her three-year old granddaughter Signe Johnson home with her and said, "I am going to raise her." And she did! Ellen, born the youngest in her family, now had a little sister.

Hard times and little available land in Sweden gave way to promises of homesteads and happiness in Canada. Rapid population growth and crop failures experienced in Sweden made the offer of a 'free' quarter of land irresistible. Ellen's parents knew it would be challenging, but they were used to hard work. Emigrating seemed a wise thing to do.

Ellen's older brother Eric began the emigration by going to Strandquist, Minnesota, U.S.A. in 1904, where he worked on the railroad and at cutting timber. In 1905, Eric moved to the Beatty area of Saskatchewan, northwest of Melfort, which was fast becoming a Swedish settlement. Two of his brothers, Jonas and Olof Artur, also emigrated to the Beatty area in 1905, where for $10 per title, they each received a homestead quarter of land.

**Ellen and Lauren Strinholm
with son Gottner**

Ellen emigrated in 1911 at the age of 22, accompanied by her older brother Nils and his wife Tekla. The trip from Sweden took almost a month. It included train travel in Sweden, three weeks on the steamer and then train travel to Melfort. The Swedish Immigration Hall located in Winnipeg provided a midway point in their train journey. Many immigrants upon arriving in Canada had the spelling of their names changed to 'the Canadian way', and Elin Karlsson became Ellen Carlson.

The following year, Ellen's parents Carl Gustaf (age 68) and Anna Lovisa Eriksson (65), their son Carl Oscar Karlsson (35) and their granddaughter Signe Johnson (15) made plans to join the family already in Canada. Carl Oscar applied for passports on March 29, 1912, and purchased tickets to sail on the luxury liner Titanic. At the time of departure on April 10, they found the Titanic had been loaded with wealthier patrons wishing to embark on its maiden voyage. The Erikssons were reassigned to the S.S. Laurentic Canadian Service Liner. It wasn't until later when they landed in Halifax on Canadian soil that they learned of the fateful sinking of the Titanic on April 14, 1912.

Meanwhile, Signe's family in Sweden, unaware of the ticket transfer, had assumed the worst. Nearly two months passed before they received word from Canada that their family members were safe. In 1913, Signe's parents and her six siblings came to Canada and settled in the Beatty area. Now all of their family was in Canada.

Ellen did housework for two different families in the Melfort area. This was customary work for most young Swedish women arriving here. And so began Ellen's ordinary, but also extraordinary life. She met a handsome man, Nels Lauren Strinholm (born in 1887) who had emigrated in 1908 from Bredtrask, Bjurholm, Sweden. He worked at logging and as a hired man on local farms and was known as a hard worker and a gentle, kind man. He had his homestead quarter, about 16 miles northwest of Melfort, and had completed breaking the 10 acres per year. Ellen and Lauren were married on January 20, 1912.

Ellen was a deeply religious person who believed in prayer, had high morals and values and a strong sense of right and wrong. Families who had been gathering in each other's homes for Bible studies by the dim light of coal-oil lamps began building a church in 1913. Mr. and Mrs. Lauren Strinholm and three other family members are listed as original members of the Swedish Mission Covenant Church at Brockington, which was dedicated in 1917.

The church was the hub of the Swedish community, helping families preserve their Swedish language and customs, and providing a social gathering place. Ellen sang a capella solos in Swedish and her brothers were also noted for their strong singing voices. Ellen was part of a very active Ladies Aid organized in 1913 to support the church financially. They held many sales and prepared many lunches and meals. The community found Sundays to be a wonderful time of gathering, good food and fellowship. This group, through their small offerings, was also able to support missionary endeavours over the years.

One of the first things Ellen and Lauren did as they began their life together was to try to learn English. They found the Eatons catalogue helpful in this task because of the pictures and short descriptions. However, Ellen preferred to speak Swedish and her children learned to speak it fluently. Later, as the children learned English at school, they shared these new words with their parents.

Lauren and Ellen Strinholm were blessed with nine children: Gottner (1913), then Folke, Myrtle, Evelyn, Clifford, Thelma, Einer, Eleanore and Lorene (1926). They were all born at home with the help of a midwife who lived on a nearby farm.

The Strinholms built a comfortable two-storey house. The first floor was the kitchen and living room. A cook stove in the kitchen and a heater in the living room kept them warm. The upstairs was one large room with three beds for the children to share. The parents slept in the living room because Ellen worried that the wood stove could cause a house fire. She monitored it closely. Later, a summer kitchen was built where all the cooking was done to help keep the house cool on summer nights.

It took many years to complete the clearing and breaking of homestead land. Their farming operation began with two oxen and a one-furrow walking plow. Eventually, horses were purchased along with other basic farm equipment for seeding and harvest. Barns and sheds were built for cattle, sheep, pigs and chickens, which was typical of the mixed farming operations of the era.

A well was dug but the water was fit only for animals. Barrels caught rain water in the summer. In winter, ice and snow was melted for drinking and household use. Lauren built an icehouse in the yard. He packed it full of ice in the winter and covered it with sawdust. The ice stayed frozen almost all summer, providing cold storage for milk, cream and food. The cold storage was not as efficient as today's refrigerators and sometimes eating tainted food was a result. They called it "summer ills." With only homemade remedies and an outhouse, a bout of food poisoning was most unpleasant.

Being a typical pioneer woman meant there was no end to the work that had to be done, but Ellen seemed to take it all in stride and was grateful that God was good to them. While always caring for babies and small children, there was cooking, baking, cleaning and tending to everything else the family required. Doing the wash was no small task. Water had to be carried in and heated on a wood stove and put into boilers. The wash was done by hand on a washboard using homemade lye soap. The clothes and sheets were wrung out by hand, then hung on the clothesline to dry. In winter, they were brought in, frozen and stiff, to finish drying. Ironing was done with heavy sad irons[11] heated on the stove.

There were many hungry children to feed. Everyone was grateful to have enough to eat. Everything was homemade: broths and soups, palt (a potato/meat dumpling), rice porridge, thin bread, cheese, butter and many loaves of bread. Animals were butchered in the fall to provide meat. Wild berries, especially blueberries and wild cranberries known as lingonberries, picked in the nearby forest (Fort à la Corne) were considered staples. The cellar was filled with many jars of canned foods, fruits and jams, along with root vegetables and potatoes. Food and water were never wasted.

As all farm women did, Ellen also had outside chores. She did garden work and looked after the cattle, pigs and chickens as well as took over all the farm chores when her husband was out in the field or working at lumber camps for extra money.

Money was always scarce. Butter and eggs were exchanged for groceries or a bit of spending money. Often butter was sold rather than cream because tubs of butter could be made and stored more easily between the trips to town. An example of ingenuity was placing eggs in a pail of oats to keep them from breaking during the wagon ride. After the eggs were exchanged for groceries, the horses had oats to eat before

---

[11] Made of cast iron, with a handle and heated in a fire; also called flat irons

returning home. By the late 1930s, egg crates with fillers became available. A 'cream truck' drove through the area picking up cans of cream and milk to take to the Melfort Creamery.

Along with the hard work, the family had to deal with many illnesses and diseases. On October 23, 1922, three-year-old Clifford became sick with influenza. Ellen stayed home with the baby and the four other children while Lauren took Clifford to the Melfort Hospital, 16 miles away, in a horse-drawn democrat (buggy). When Lauren arrived there, the doctor said he would need $30 before he would examine Clifford. The bank was closed and Lauren did not have that much cash. While Clifford waited in a hospital chair, Lauren went to a friend's house to borrow some money. When he returned, he was told that little Clifford had died while he was gone. Everyone was crushed when Lauren returned home with Clifford's lifeless body.

In July 1926, a few months after the birth of their youngest child Lorene, Lauren became ill following a tonsillectomy. He developed a lung condition suspected to be tuberculosis and was sent to the Fort Qu'Appelle Sanitorium in southern Saskatchewan for treatment, where he had to stay for more than a year. The patients' beds were wheeled out to an unheated veranda because it was believed sunshine could heal tuberculosis. Lauren found the cold difficult to bear, so Ellen knit socks and mitts for him to wear.

Later it was discovered that instead of TB, Lauren had an abscessed lung and he was released from the sanitorium. Lauren was transferred by train to the newly built St. Paul's Hospital in Saskatoon for surgery. He was in Saskatoon for almost two weeks. During this time, Ellen tried to travel by horse and democrat to Melfort, where she planned to catch the train to Saskatoon, but her young untrained horses were uncooperative. To further complicate matters, a lot of snow fell early that fall, the potatoes and carrots had to be dug, and there were more than 20 acres of oats and wheat to put through the binder. Ellen was exhausted after helping her sons stack and haul 30 loads of hay home with horse and wagon. She also had eight children to care for, ranging in age from 14 years to 14 months. Sadly, Lauren died in Saskatoon on September 28, 1927, at the age of 40, without ever seeing any of his family again.

After her husband died, Ellen took her oldest sons Gottner and Folke out of school during Grade 8 to help manage the family farm. Einer, the youngest son, was taken out of school during Grade 7 to help with seeding. There was so much work to be done on the farm that the boys never returned to school. It was difficult work with teams of four horses needed to pull the two-furrow plow, the harrows and seeder. Occasionally, a man was hired to help in spring and fall, but money was always scarce. Sometimes Ellen traded seed for lumber.

In 1929, Ellen purchased a car for her family. It was a used 1926 Essex, two-door coupe with wooden spokes in the wheels. Then the Depression years of the 1930s hit. The price of wheat dropped so low, it would not even cover the cost of threshing. Neighbours who had purchased new cars were returning them. Ellen wished she had never bought hers.

Ellen carried on with sheer determination, a deep personal faith in God, the help of her older children and the kindness of family and neighbours. Her children were everything to her and she devoted her life to them. Through it all, she maintained a positive outlook and did whatever she could to provide for her family. Her children said that although she was small of stature, she worked as hard as any man. While she had a quiet manner, no one doubted or challenged their mother's authority.

Ellen sheared sheep, washed and carded the wool and spun it on a spinning wheel. She knitted mittens, scarves, socks and sweaters. Almost all basic necessities were handmade. Flour sacks became pillowcases, dishtowels or bloomers for the girls. Ellen was careful to not have the name 'Robin Hood' on the bloomers. Clothes were mended, collars and cuffs were turned, and some clothes were re-made. When new suits, clothes and shoes had to be purchased, the older boys and girls got the new outfits. Their old clothing was handed down to the younger children, who were not always pleased to receive it. Anything not wearable was made into quilts or blankets. Floor mats were made on a loom and a bag was filled with scraps to be used as cleaning rags.

Even though the family worked hard, there were always opportunities for teasing and playing jokes. They sang together, yodelled and even whistled while they worked! They made their own fun and played many games together. One of their favourite winter pastimes was meeting Signe's children at a huge straw stack (left from the threshing machine) for 'downhill skiing' on their homemade skis. Einer also made a set of 'dual' stilts, which could be turned over to walk either at 4½ feet or six feet tall. The children learned to play the pump organ, guitar and violin. Two daughters learned to play a 32-string autoharp. The children enjoyed singing in church as well. Sunday meetings at church and Christmas concerts were special times.

Ellen's life had always been closely tied to Signe Johnson. In 1915, Signe married Carl Valentine (pronounced Volenteen) Strinholm, a brother to Ellen's husband Lauren. The families lived a half mile apart and their lives became almost inseparable. In 1924, Signe's daughter Margaret became desperately ill. Ellen took Signe's other four children home with her to look after them. It was found that Margaret had diphtheria so she and her parents were quarantined. The antibiotic for diphtheria had been developed but was not available in rural Saskatchewan. Margaret passed away at four years of age.

The struggles and hardships continued for Ellen. Her father had died in 1915 from pneumonia and after that, her mother lived in the homes of each of her children. In 1931, Ellen's mother Anna Lovisa suffered a stroke and was left bedridden, paralyzed and unable to speak. Ellen placed a bed in her living room so her mother could still be a part of family life. Ellen slept on the sofa in the living room to be near her mother. Ellen cared tenderly for her mother for a year. Anna Lovisa had a second stroke and passed away on March 25, 1932, at age 85.

On a very cold night in January 1932, Ellen's children were wakened by their mother's scream. "Signe's house is on fire!" Signe was six months pregnant and her husband was away logging on the North Saskatchewan River. Ellen's family jumped out of bed and could see the flames a half mile away. Ellen, Gottner and Folke rushed outside to help just as Signe's daughter Millie arrived with the youngest children on their horse-drawn toboggan. Signe had awakened to find the attic in flames. She woke the children and took them to the barn where they dressed. Five-year-old Elma, tired and cold, had crawled back into bed during the turmoil. Signe managed to get her out for the second time.

Ellen, Signe and her daughter Lillian (14) gathered as many possessions as possible before the house was completely engulfed in flames. Meanwhile, the youngest children from both families watched the fire from the safety of Ellen's living room window. The next day, Ellen sent Folke (18) with a team of two horses and a cutter to find Signe's husband Valentine and bring him home.

During this time, 19 people were staying at Ellen's home with makeshift beds all over the floor. She must have handled it very well, because the children thought this was fun. Valentine began working on fixing up the summer kitchen so his family would have a place to live.

On May 8, 1932, Signe gave birth to daughter Mildred. Unfortunately, there were complications during the delivery and Signe never recovered, passing away on June 16, leaving behind her husband and eight children. Ellen took care of the baby for the first five weeks of the baby's life. She made a bed for Mildred by setting a drawer on two chairs. Ellen welcomed Signe's children to come and see their baby sister at any time.

It was Signe's wish that after the funeral, Signe's brother Arthur and his wife Nannie take the new baby. They had previously lost their only child, and they raised Mildred as their own. For a few years, the younger children went to live with Valentine's sisters and their families. It was a sad time for the family.

On May 19, 1938, Signe's husband Valentine died from cancer. Signe's children had now lost both parents. That spring, the three oldest children – Millie (19), Lillian (18) and Lawrence (17) – were determined to keep the family together on the farm. On October 8, 1938, Einer was outside in the yard when he heard screams coming from Signe's yard. He told Ellen, and she and her family began running down the road. They met up with Signe's children who were coming to tell them Lawrence had fallen into the ice well and had drowned. He had tried to retrieve an axe from the well but when he climbed onto the ladder inside it, the first two rungs broke. It seemed he had fallen backward and hit his head on the well cribbing. His sisters and younger brother were busy milking cows and doing chores and had not seen it happen.

Ellen sent Einer to a farm that had a phone, to call for help. He ran frantically for a mile and a half in the dark, zigzagging through the bush. Lawrence was a big brother to both families, and Einer's best friend. The loss was enormous. This was one time when Ellen was completely overwhelmed. She threw her hands toward heaven and asked God, "What is going to happen to this family?"

Ellen was like a mother to Signe's children and the parent figure to both families. Christmases were spent at her house with all the children feeling like they were brother and sister. Signe's daughter Elma often stayed at Ellen's house and once, when she was about 14 years old, asked Aunt Ellen what her mother had looked like. Ellen went upstairs and brought down a mirror. She told Elma to look into it. Ellen said, "This is what your mother looked like." Elma was very happy to hear that.

Gottner, the oldest son, remained at home with Ellen after all the other children went out on their own. Gottner built a new house in 1950, with all the new conveniences of the day including electricity and telephones. Ellen lived in that house for only a year before her heart gave out. As she lay in the hospital bed with her children around her, she encouraged them to live for the Lord. Ellen died on December 30, 1951.

Ellen's legacy to her children was that, through it all, they became caring, kind, responsible people who genuinely liked and supported each other throughout their lives. She had raised a happy family with a positive outlook and a sense of purpose. Her family remained very closely-knit, most of them living and raising their families within a few miles of their original home. Ellen epitomized the true pioneer spirit. To her, it was just her life. To her family, it was a life that deserves recognition, honour and respect. She is an inspiration to her descendants.

By Deb Strinholm-Klassen, granddaughter (daughter of Einer) and Pauline Johnson, granddaughter (daughter-in-law of Myrtle)

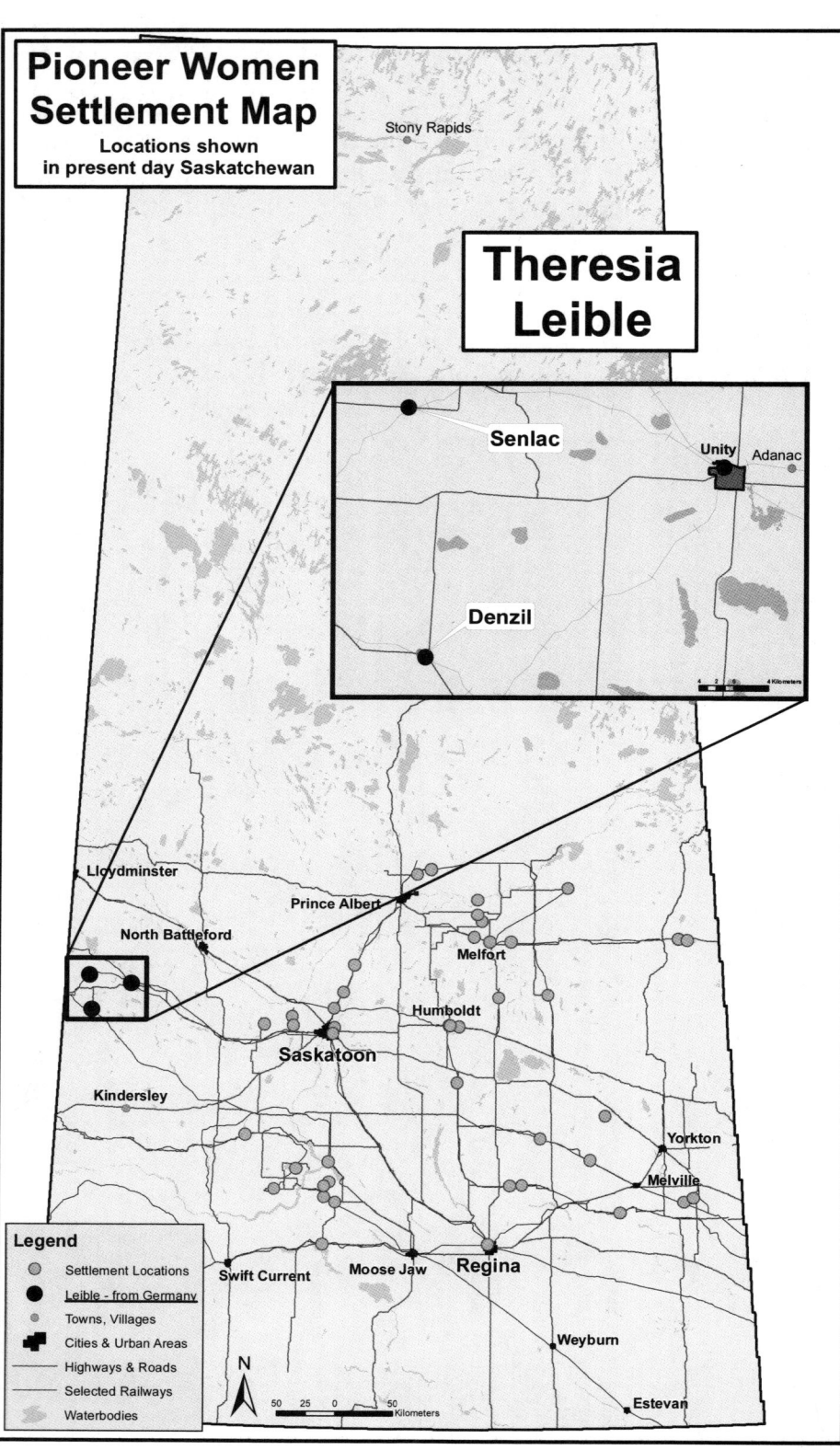

THERESIA LEIBLE
(1889-1968)

Theresia was born on October 8, 1889, in Durbach, Germany to Heinrich Benz and Viktoria Lang. She married Alexander Lauinger on May 2, 1914. The First World War had just begun. Hardships for Theresia started early, living through the turmoil of war with the death of a seven-month-old son and the death of her husband in the last week of the war.

On May 4, 1920, Theresia married Andreas Leible in Durbach, Germany. Over the next six years, Theresia worked as a midwife in their town. During this time, she gave birth to three children: Hilda (1921), Andreas (1923) and Heinrich (1925).

Due to the Great Depression, cost of living and a lack of work in Germany, the family decided to move to Canada. In April 1926, Andreas travelled to Canada in search of a homestead for his family. He had only $50 in his pocket. Months later, on a cool September day, Theresia packed up their three young children and their belongings and went to Liverpool, England to board the ship Montrose. Families were only allowed to bring their personal belongings, bedding and dishes with them.

Imagine the hardship of travelling with three children on a ship for several weeks, encountering seasickness, dysentery and restricted space, not to mention the sanitation concerns and food rations. Theresia must have had mixed feelings, bouncing back and forth between the fear of the unknown and the desire to be reunited with her husband.

Theresia Leible after collecting eggs

They arrived in Montreal, Quebec, in their new country on October 9, 1926, but there was still a long way to go to reach their destination. With language barriers, luggage, all their belongings, one child in her arms and two holding her hands, Theresia managed to get on the train that would take them safely to Denzil, Saskatchewan. She was a courageous, determined and strong woman to venture on such a journey with only $20 in her possession. This was the beginning of her life as a pioneer woman in Saskatchewan.

In 1931, after working for farmers and renting land in the Denzil area, Theresia and Andreas bought a section of natural prairie land in the Senlac area from the Hudson Bay Company. Since no ground was broken and there were no buildings on the land, they stayed with a neighbour who lived one mile away and walked to the land every day to till the soil and work on a wooden granary for a temporary dwelling. The tilling was done with horse and plow. The building was constructed with handsaws. In 1932, they built a sod house into the side of a hill, where they raised their family.

It was hard work getting a crop growing, especially when the Dirty Thirties came and dust storms left dust drifts similar in size to modern-day snow drifts. When they did get a good crop, they hauled it by horse and wagon about 20 kilometres to the closest elevator, shovelling the grain on and off by hand. All transportation was done by horse until 1942 when they bought their first automobile. In 1946, they purchased their first tractor.

The winters were harsh with plenty of snow and cold and no electricity. They heated their home with wood and woke up each morning to find their water bucket frozen over. One can imagine the emotions that went through Theresia's mind as she lit the fire in the stove to put some breakfast on the table for her family. "Will we have enough food to survive until we can get to town again? Did I make the right decision, leaving a country so advanced compared to this wilderness they call the Prairies of Saskatchewan? Will my family prosper? Will I ever see my homeland again?"

On May 16, 1938, Andreas and the children became Canadian citizens. Theresia was granted Canadian citizenship on June 13, 1939.

Theresia and Andreas managed to build a successful farming enterprise, adding more buildings on their land. In 1947, they built a hip-roofed barn into the side of a hill, a feat of which they were very proud. The loft of this barn had ground-level access on the high side of the hill and was later used for neighbourhood dances.

In 1951, after 20 years of building their homestead from prairie sod, they left their married son Henry to take over the homestead and they moved to a vacant farm nearby, where they planned their retirement. In November 1952, Theresia and Andreas made a memorable trip back to Germany to see some of the relatives and friends they had left behind about 26 years earlier. They stayed in Germany, visiting until March 1953. Later that year, they bought a house in Unity. They finally had the luxury of electricity when the power was brought into the rural area in the mid 1950s. They kept a beautiful flower garden and orchard and made wine from the fruit. They also looked after the orchards at the local hospital grounds and kept bees, selling the honey. This helped subsidize their retirement years, enjoyed with family and friends.

In 1967, Theresia's health started to fail and on April 8, 1968, she passed away. Pleasant View Cemetery is the final resting place of one of Saskatchewan's brave pioneer women.

By David Kiefer, grandson, and Rose Marie Normand, granddaughter (children of Hilda)

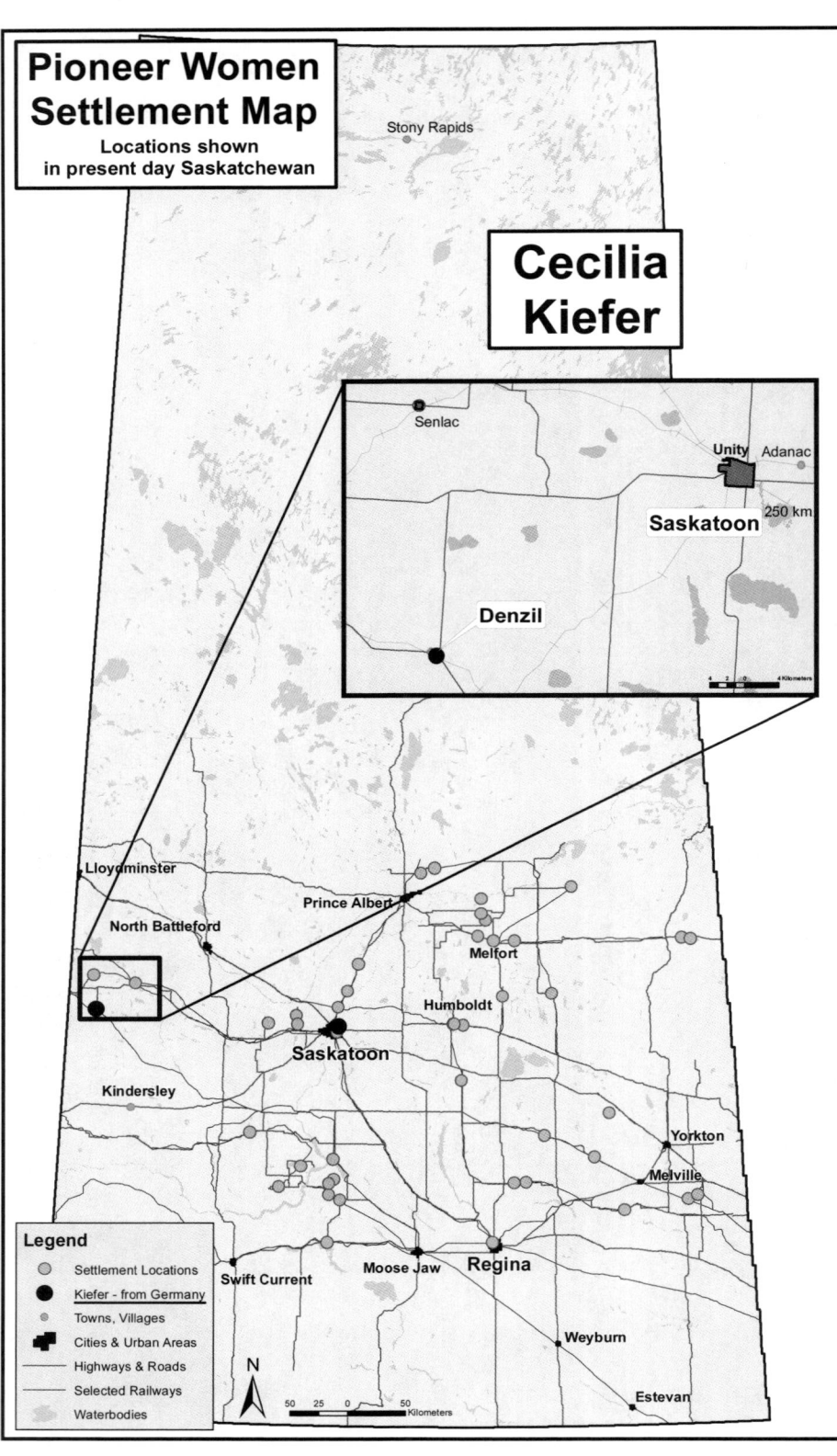

Cecilia Kiefer
(1892-1978)

Cecilia was born on October 21, 1892, to Franz Xaver Sandhaas and Theresia Vogt in the town of Durbach, Germany. She married Joseph Kiefer on September 25, 1916, and their two sons, Joseph and Robert, were born in Durbach.

In April 1927, Cecilia's husband immigrated to Canada in search of a better life. He only had $10 in his pocket but began to prepare to bring his family to this new country. In late September, Cecilia packed up the only things she was allowed to bring to Canada – her two sons, a few personal belongings, some bedding and their dishes. But then, the most devastating event occurred.

For health reasons, Cecilia's nine-year-old Joseph was not allowed by Canadian immigration to travel to Canada. He had been born with a major hearing deficit and for this reason, Canadian immigration laws prevented him from being accepted into Canada.

Cecilia had to decide whether to stay in Germany with her sons or go to be with her husband who was waiting for her in Canada. She was devastated, but made the decision to leave her oldest son behind with relatives in Germany. The positive side of this painful decision was that Joseph was sent to a special school for the deaf in Heidelberg, Germany. He would not have received this type of education in Canada in 1927.

With a heavy heart, Cecilia took her second son, seven-year-old Robert, and boarded the ship Empress of France at Hamburg, Germany and began the long trip across

Cecilia Kiefer (right) with a neighbour

the ocean. They arrived in Quebec, Canada on October 8, 1927, with $40 tucked inside Cecilia's purse. A little less than two weeks later, Cecilia turned 35. From Quebec, they took a train to Saskatchewan to meet Joseph. He had rented a parcel of land at Denzil, about 150 kilometres southwest of North Battleford.

The family lived in a one-room house until an addition could be built a couple years later. Cecilia worked hard to break land for a small garden. A team of horses helped with ploughing their small parcel of land. Soon they also owned chickens, pigs and a couple of cows. Cecilia sold the eggs to buy items they could not produce or raise on the farm, such as sugar, salt and flour. Empty flour sacks were used for making clothing or towels.

Then the 1930s struck. There was reason for calling that era the Dirty Thirties. Surviving the dust bowl of those years was a challenge. Everything was rationed ... as if things weren't tough enough already. Those years took a toll on many. Some families left their farms and moved to the cities to look for work. Often, there was no work there either.

For Cecilia and Joseph, life on the farm continued to be full of long days of hard work. Helping shovel a load of grain onto a wagon pulled by a team of horses and taking it to the closest elevator about 25 kilometres away took a good part of a day. After buying some supplies in town and giving the horses a rest, they made the long trip back to a cold house. Cecilia then had to get the fire going in the wood stove to warm up the house and to make a meal for the family. The only electricity available at the time was 12-volt electricity created by charging batteries with wind power. This was a precious resource and was used only for lighting in the evening.

There must have been many times when Cecilia thought about packing up her few possessions and moving back to Germany, where her oldest son was living. The determination to survive and make a better life for her family kept her strong.

In 1934, Cecilia and Joseph travelled to Germany in an attempt to bring back the son they had left behind. Young Joseph was now 16 years old, had established friendships and employment there and did not wish to move to Canada. Cecilia and Joseph stayed for several weeks but returned to Canada without their oldest son.

In 1939, when the Second World War broke out, it brought another huge cross for Cecilia to bear. Her husband Joseph, being of German heritage, was taken to two different detention camps in Canada for the duration of the war and Cecilia was left to keep their farm going with the help of her then-19-year-old son Robert. Thoughts of the son left behind in Germany were constantly with her during this period. Hard work and a strong faith, including daily prayers, helped Cecilia get through that time.

During all the hardships in her life, Cecilia remained positive and never complained. She kept her anxieties and emotional hurts to herself.

While the war was on, the landowners expressed interest in selling the land and Robert purchased it to begin his life as a married man. Cecilia continued to work on the farm with him. Joseph was released from the detention camp in 1944 near the end of the war to attend his son's wedding.

After Robert married, Cecilia and Joseph moved to Saskatoon, 250 kilometres east of Denzil. Joseph built homes and did carpentry work while Cecilia continued to be the homemaker. She loved to garden and always had beautiful flowers and a few fruit trees. When Cecilia and Joseph Kiefer celebrated their 60th wedding anniversary in 1976, Cecilia's own home-grown flowers provided the beautiful table decorations for their diamond anniversary celebration at St. John Bosco Roman Catholic Church in Saskatoon, of which they were active members.

Although Cecilia had a difficult life, she always had a strong faith and a ready smile. She was well loved by her grandchildren, whom she showered with love and affection.

On November 22, 1978, Cecilia was called to her final resting place. She is buried in Saskatoon's Woodlawn Cemetery among other courageous pioneer women of Saskatchewan.

By David Kiefer, grandson, and Rose Marie Normand, granddaughter (children of Robert)

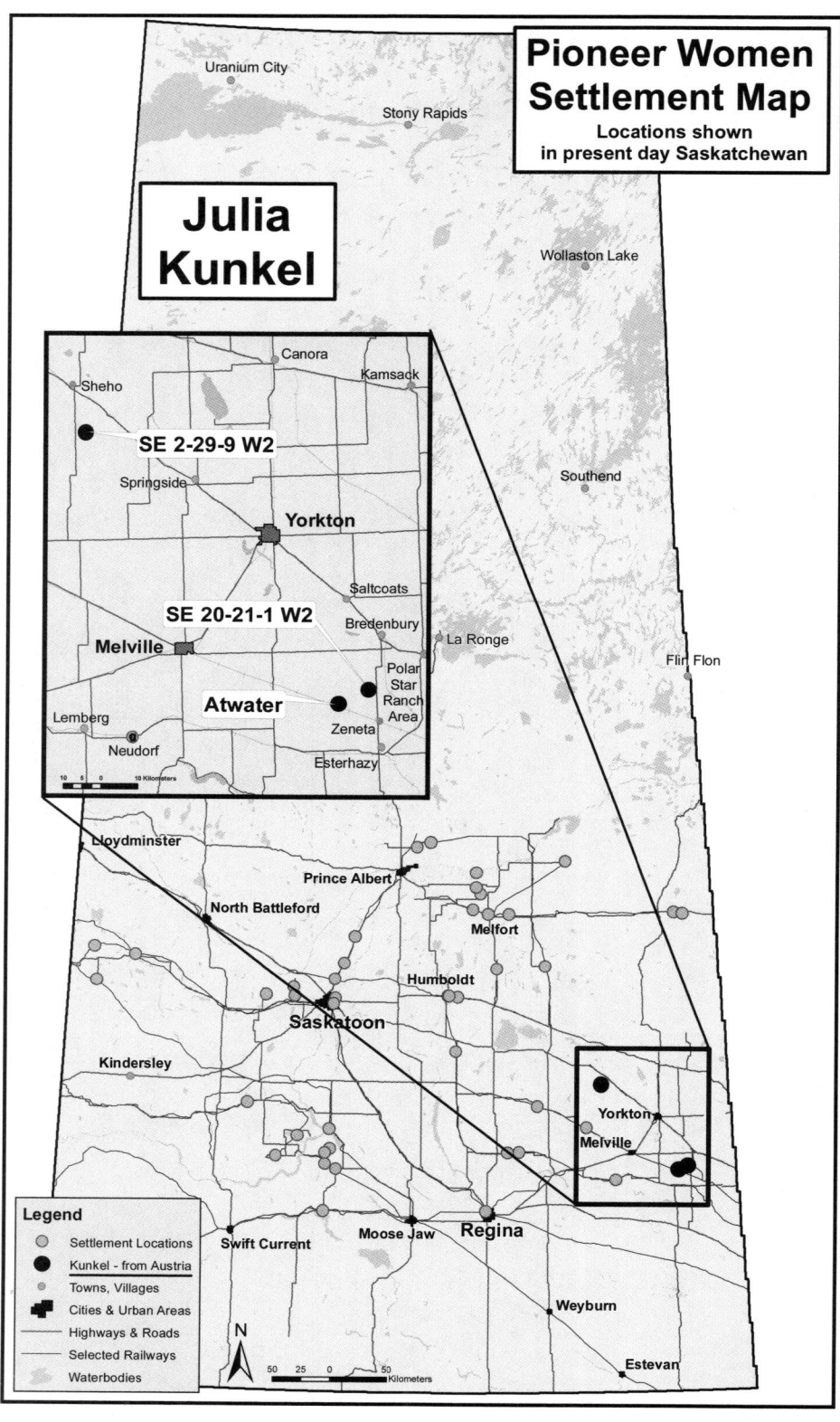

Julia Kunkel
(1892-1968)

Julia was born on December 2, 1892, in Lemberg (L'viv) Galicia, former Habsburg Empire. Her father, Phillip Müller, arrived in Canada in March 1897 to acquire a homestead near Ellisboro, Assiniboia, North-West Territories. He built a 24-foot by 16-foot soddie[12] house and had it ready for his family's arrival a few months later.

Five-year-old Julia, her mother Karolina and her brother Jacob braved a two-week ocean voyage to make a new life and a new family in Canada. They disembarked from the vessel Armenia at the port of Montreal, Quebec on October 14, 1897. Their arrival in Canada was at a time when travel was difficult and settlement was taking place in Western Canada. North-West Territories roads were nonexistent and consisted of wheel ruts from Point A to Point B. They began farming on the homestead in 1898 with the oxen team plowing the soil to prepare the land for its first crop.

Julia's childhood consisted of attending school in the Rosewood district, which was a district away from their home, due to the shortage of teachers. Julia also helped work on the farm, which was hard work for a young immigrant wanting to become a Canadian.

Julia's siblings were Jacob (Jake), Karolina Emilie, Lydia Katherine, Fred, Frieda and Elsa. While growing up, there was much to do such as washing clothes by hand and milking cows morning and night. In spring, a big garden was planted and it required watering and weeding throughout the summer. The family picked strawberries, saskatoons and gooseberries to

---

[12] Term used by settlers as a reference to a sod-built house

Julia Kunkel

make preserves. Since there were no refrigerators or freezers, canning of cucumbers, carrots and beets was required to have vegetables through the winter. Potatoes were also harvested and readied for storage.

Fall was very busy with the harvesting and bagging of grain. The grain was then loaded on the wagon or sleigh to make the 16-mile trip to the elevator located in Wolseley or Grenfell. This trip involved loading all the bags, travelling to the edge of the Qu'Appelle Valley and unloading half of the bags at the bottom of the hill. Half of the bags were then driven to the top on the other side of the hill and unloaded from the wagon or sleigh. Then the wagon came back down the hill to pick up the remaining bags at the bottom, turn around and travel back up to the top of the hill, where the previously unloaded bags were picked up and the trip was continued, on to the elevator with the full load.

Education was limited and all work was done by hand. All the clothing was homemade using a treadle sewing machine.

Home remedies included a mixture of onions boiled in honey for coughs, a tablespoon of Zeagles magnet oil[13] as a cure for sore throats and Castoria[14] for whatever else ailed a person. A homemade recipe for tapeworm called for ingredients shipped from Germany to Regina. All these homemade remedies were shared with others in the community who needed help because doctors and hospitals were many miles away. With the great distances to travel to see a doctor, people commonly died from incidents such as a ruptured appendicitis.

Julia married Henry Bender on July 25, 1911. They had five children: George Heinrich, Otto Johann, Emma Ida, Joseph and Margaret Christina.

Julia was particularly close to and proud of her brother Jacob (Jake), who enlisted in January 1914 in the Canadian army with the 45th Battalion. After training, he was shipped overseas to France in March and was posted to the Canadian Mounted Rifles. Jake took part in several major battles and was awarded the Meritorious Service medal, coming home to Neudorf, SK in 1919 as a Canadian hero.

Julia's mother Karolina died on November 29, 1918, from influenza. Julia's husband Henry Bender also died during the influenza epidemic on June 10, 1920.

Julia married Gustaf Kunkel on November 16, 1920, in Neudorf, Saskatchewan. The two families were blended as one and exist today in mutual respect and understanding. Children of Gustaf and Julia Kunkel are: Arthur Phillip, Gertrude Frieda, Curtis (Curt) Fredric and William Karl.

From 1890 to the early 1900s, Neudorf and Lemberg had a large number of residents who had immigrated to Canada from Galicia and Volhynia, an area of modern-day Ukraine. Churches and schools were built mainly with volunteer help by the immigrant settlers. Neudorf was officially incorporated as a village in 1907. A hotel was constructed in 1907 and a pharmacy was built and opened in 1907. The Canadian Pacific Railway line was built at Neudorf in 1904.

Julia encouraged her children to attend church on a regular basis. Catechism lessons were taught at home. Travel to attend church services was done by horse and sleigh or buggy and

---

[13] Taken with sugar in a teaspoon to make it palatable for children
[14] A brand of castor oil

was always something to enjoy. First, the family attended St. John's Church south of Neudorf and later they went to the former Evangelical Lutheran Church, Synod of Ohio, now known as Christ Lutheran Church. Confirmation classes were undertaken by the church pastor and included German language lessons in the summer. Education was important and was not taken lightly. The children attended the one-room Baber Public School from Grades 1 to 10 and often saw and learned from lessons a grade ahead of their grade.

In March 1946, the Kunkel family relocated from the Neudorf district to a farm near Atwater, Saskatchewan. This homestead was formerly known as part of the Polar Star Ranch.

Chickens were grown 'free range' during the summer months and were mainly used for bartering and selling of eggs. There were no hatcheries in the early years. Hens were carefully selected to sit on the eggs to hatch or to incubate the eggs to the chick stage, with one hen hatching approximately eight to 10 eggs. Hens in hatching mode were called clucks. Incubation time line is 21 days for chicks and 28 days for ducks and turkeys. It was a welcome sight when the hens emerged with a brood of chicks. Occasionally, a family of chicks would be hatched by a hen that had hidden the nest. This was always a bonus when this hen arrived with another brood of chicks.

Eggs and chickens were a daily staple for settlers, used in various forms including hard-boiled eggs and devilled eggs for picnics. Roasted chicken with vegetables and homemade gravy made up the most common meal served for Sunday supper or for a threshing crew of hungry men. Eggs were boiled and coloured to celebrate Easter, which was a happy occasion on the farm.

The chicken flock was generally protected by keeping the birds close to the farmyard. A stray fox at times got a free dinner or a marauding skunk sometimes got into the chicken house at night and did some damage to the flock. This did not happen without a lot of barking by the family dog trying to wake up the whole family to stop the scavenging skunk. When a hawk flying overhead alerted the flock of imminent danger, the clucks used the clucking sound to alert their chicks. The chicks then either squatted down and sat very still or ran directly to their mother cluck for protection. In most instances, the chicks hid under the cluck's wings until another clucking sounded that all was safe again.

Gustaf and Julia retired from the farm in 1949 and built a home in Atwater, where they spent many hours enjoying their vegetable and flower gardens. Julia died on June 23, 1968. She is buried in the Lutheran Cemetery at Atwater. The farm continued to be in the Kunkel family until 2008.

By Curt Kunkel, son, and Ron Kunkel, grandson (son of Curt)

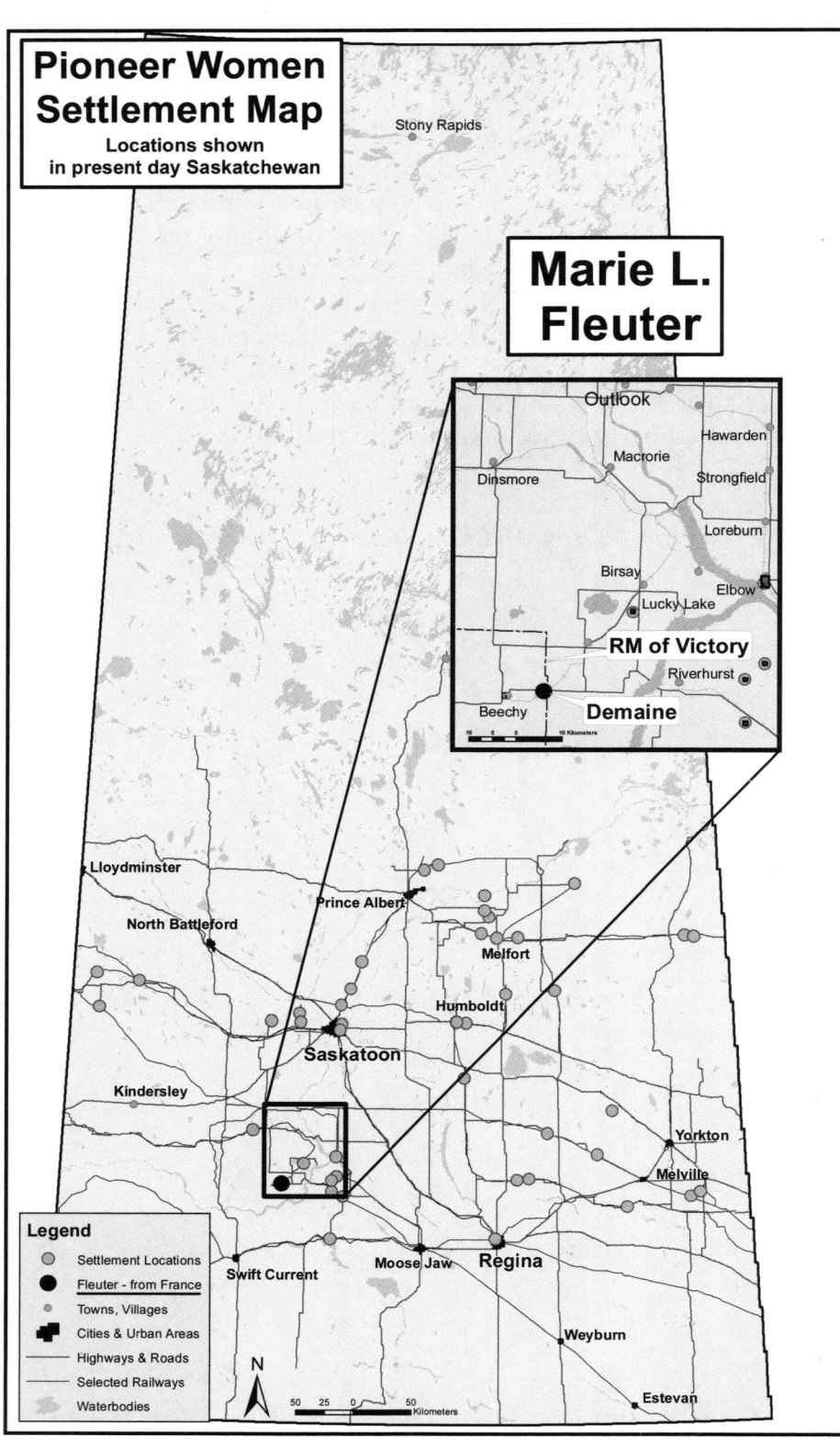

Marie L. Fleuter
(1893-1976)

Marie Louise Lamande was born on May 9, 1893, in the Finistère district of France. On April 30, 1919, she married Victor Joseph Fleuter, a neighbour who lived seven miles down the road. Victor had purchased a homestead in Saskatchewan 12 years earlier and was anxious to bring his new wife back to Canada with him.

In 1905, Victor had immigrated to Canada from his home on a small farm in France, hoping for a better life. He worked for several months in what became the Demaine district of Saskatchewan and became the first homesteader to take up permanent residence in the rural municipality of Victory. On June 17, 1906, Victor filed for the homestead rights to his land. Less than a year later, on April 21, 1907, he proved his 160 acres of virgin prairie in central Saskatchewan. He built a sod shack and barn, dug a shallow well and plowed the land to ensure his future in Canada. The Dominion Lands/Homestead Act at the time specified that at least 10 acres be cultivated each summer in order to 'prove up', breaking and working the land.

In the summer of 1914, war broke out in Europe and Victor offered to report for duty with the French army. He gave his favourite horse and his little dog Sandy a special goodbye and was on the front lines before the year was out. Victor was wounded and taken prisoner in 1915. Although truce was declared on November 11, 1918, it was well into 1919 before the prisoners were on their way home. Victor spent the winter

Marie Louise Fleuter

regaining his health and becoming reacquainted with family and friends, including Louise.

On May 22, 1919, less than a month after their wedding, Louise and Victor left France for their new life together in Canada. This was a very exciting journey for Louise since she had never seen the ocean before, even though it was only 28 miles from her home in France.

They arrived by train at Waldeck, Saskatchewan and then travelled by car the rest of the way to their new home. They drove up the river hills from the Herbert Ferry and searched the horizon to the north until Victor's home came into view.

When Victor returned home from the war, many of his possessions had been distributed amongst the neighbours as they had feared the loss of his life. Most were voluntarily returned with the return of Victor to the area.

For Louise, life in this new land was quite different. There were many things to learn – baking, sewing and especially speaking, reading and writing a new language. Among her first visitors were two of the Demaine girls, neighbours to the northwest whose father was the town's namesake. They knew Victor well and wanted to meet his pretty wife. They spoke no French and Louise spoke little English, so they smiled a lot, drank tea and became friends.

The Home Loving Hearts section of the *Free Press Prairie Farmer* was used in an interesting way to help Louise with her English. She read the letters out loud to her husband, not knowing what the words meant, and he interpreted them. There were many laughs about her pronunciation but she learned easily, so her progress was good. Victor spoke three languages and had command of a fourth – Breton, French, English and German – however he could not read or write any of those languages. Therefore the job of farm correspondent was eventually taken over from the neighbours by Louise. She had only three years of schooling in the old country, beginning at age eight and taking two grades a year. Later on, when her children were doing their homework in a haphazard manner, she often told them that she learned more in those three years than they were learning in eight.

Another of Louise's accomplishments was that of making excellent bread, but it was not so in the beginning. Several near-failures did little for her reputation in the kitchen. Exasperated when yet another batch refused to rise, Louise took the pan of dough outside and stuffed it down a gopher hole. The next day was a lovely sunny day. Looking out the south window from the dinner table, her husband noticed an unusual flower rising up through the grass. "Come and see," he said. Louise took one look. "Mon pain!" she exclaimed, and laughed with embarrassment at the rising bread dough.

Life in the 1920s was generally happy and very busy. Three more quarters of land were acquired and seven children were born: Joseph (1920); Marie; Victor; Henry; Arthur; George and Georgette (1927).

With more land, it soon became apparent that the tractor must replace the faithful horse. This meant much new machinery. The bumper crop of 1928 assured that improvement, as did the numerous salesmen who roamed the countryside that fall. Farmers found themselves deep in debt, however, when the market crash came in 1929. They were a very worried lot, with Victor among them. Prices hit rock bottom and gave very little indication of improving as the Dirty Thirties came along. Collectors now appeared everywhere with their black briefcases and unsmiling faces. The future looked very bleak and uncertain. With seven young children to think about, it was a very anxious time. As fate would have it, the load was not to be Victor's. He died trying to rescue his oldest son Joseph, who had fallen through the ice while going for a forbidden skate on the nearby dam. Joseph also lost his life on that fateful day of November 14, 1931.

The years that followed were difficult ones for Louise. She and the children remained on the farm with the help of her brother Pete Lamande, who moved from his farm nearby to live with them.

Drought settled over the Prairies, so crops were poor and prices for products had fallen to an all-time low. Sheer grit and determination carried most people through and it also helped to pocket one's pride and ask for assistance when things got really bad. When the drought hit and there was no food, seed grain, clothing or coal, the family applied for relief with the municipal office. Similar to a loan, it had to be repaid.

The Widow's Allowance was available from the government upon application and this was necessary the year there was no crop at all. It, too, had to be repaid and a record had to be kept of where every dollar was spent – a most unnecessary chore since the monthly cheque seldom covered the basic needs of Louise's growing family. Luxuries were unknown. She finally threw away the scribbler she kept for record keeping. The current inspector asked no questions. In general, they could see she was doing her best, though there were those who might have been better in other occupations. It was a red-letter day when she no longer needed assistance and was able to write and tell them so.

On the farm, there was usually a good supply of milk and butter, though occasionally this was not so. The school sandwiches were then 'buttered' with lard and the children were cautioned not to tell this to anyone for fear of being teased. The boys had a little song they sang on those mornings: "Bread and lard, to make you hard." They sang this over and over while they got ready for school, perhaps not realizing how bad it was for their mother's morale. So much for stigmas!

Warm clothing for the family was a different situation. Every fall after each of the creditors got a little portion of the crop (if any was available), an order was placed for winter clothes. The $5-per-child Children's Allowance didn't buy too much – not nearly the quantity or quality for the harsh prairie winters. A trip to Beechy one cold fall day did wonders to alleviate that problem. After making the rounds of stopping at the municipal office to see about relief coal, buying a few groceries and a can of coal oil and a couple pairs of overshoes for the children, there was only $5 left in Louise's worn black purse. It was starting to snow but Louise just had to have one more look in the window of Santy's store. She had earlier seen a little machine in there that looked like it could be used for spinning. She used to spin in the old country. Maybe it was still there. It was! And the price was exactly $5!

That little machine was worth its weight in gold. Everyone in the family soon had warm socks and mitts, then sweaters and later, the fine long fleece from the young sheep was spun into a soft yarn and made into two-piece underwear for the boys. It was never a chore for Louise to spin and knit. Instead, it was a deep comfort for her to know that the family would now be warm.

A very low period came for the family in the winter of 1936. It was an extremely harsh winter. The snow was deep and the cold severe. The red measles were going around and all the children were very sick. Georgette's appendix ruptured. Though she was flown to Saskatoon, she died just before her ninth birthday. Worn and weary, Louise became seriously ill with pneumonia. There were no miracle drugs, but mustard plasters[15] twice a day were probably what saved her. The help of kindly neighbours brought cheer and courage. So when the spring winds blew warm, after a month in bed, Louise rose, pale and weak, to face another year.

---

[15] Spread on a cloth and usually used on the chest to fight congestion

The future finally brought prosperity, hand in hand with the war of 1939. Debts were gradually taken care of and from then on, if items were purchased they were paid for immediately. If something was not needed, it was not purchased. After the drought broke, money was available for an irrigation system for the garden.

The 1940s brought a trip back to the homeland, by boat because "flying was too dangerous." After 29 years, Louise found many changes, which she was more or less prepared for, brought about by war as well as time. Many family members and friends were gone. The weather was considerably warmer than that of the Prairies, however. With no central heating, houses felt damp and cool to Louise. So after making the rounds and having a good visit with all, she was ready to come home, feeling satisfied that Saskatchewan was a pretty good part of the world in which to live.

Grandchildren were important in Louise's life. She had 10 in all, with eight living nearby, so Granny was a significant part in each of their lives. Three of her children married: Art, Hank and Marie. George died on December 1, 1960, at the age of 33 after a long illness. Vic remained single, living on the family farm.

In early 1963, Louise moved from the farm into Beechy for the winter, but enjoyed spending time on the farm in the summer. In 1969, an ulcerated leg required extra care and treatment, so she moved into the Pioneer Lodge at Outlook on February 19. She resided there until her death on August 31, 1976 at the age of 83. And so the final chapter in the story of her life came to a close. These few anecdotes hopefully convey to the reader an insight into her personality as her family saw her – generous and giving, sturdy and rugged, independent and wise.

By Marie (Fleuter) Moebis, daughter

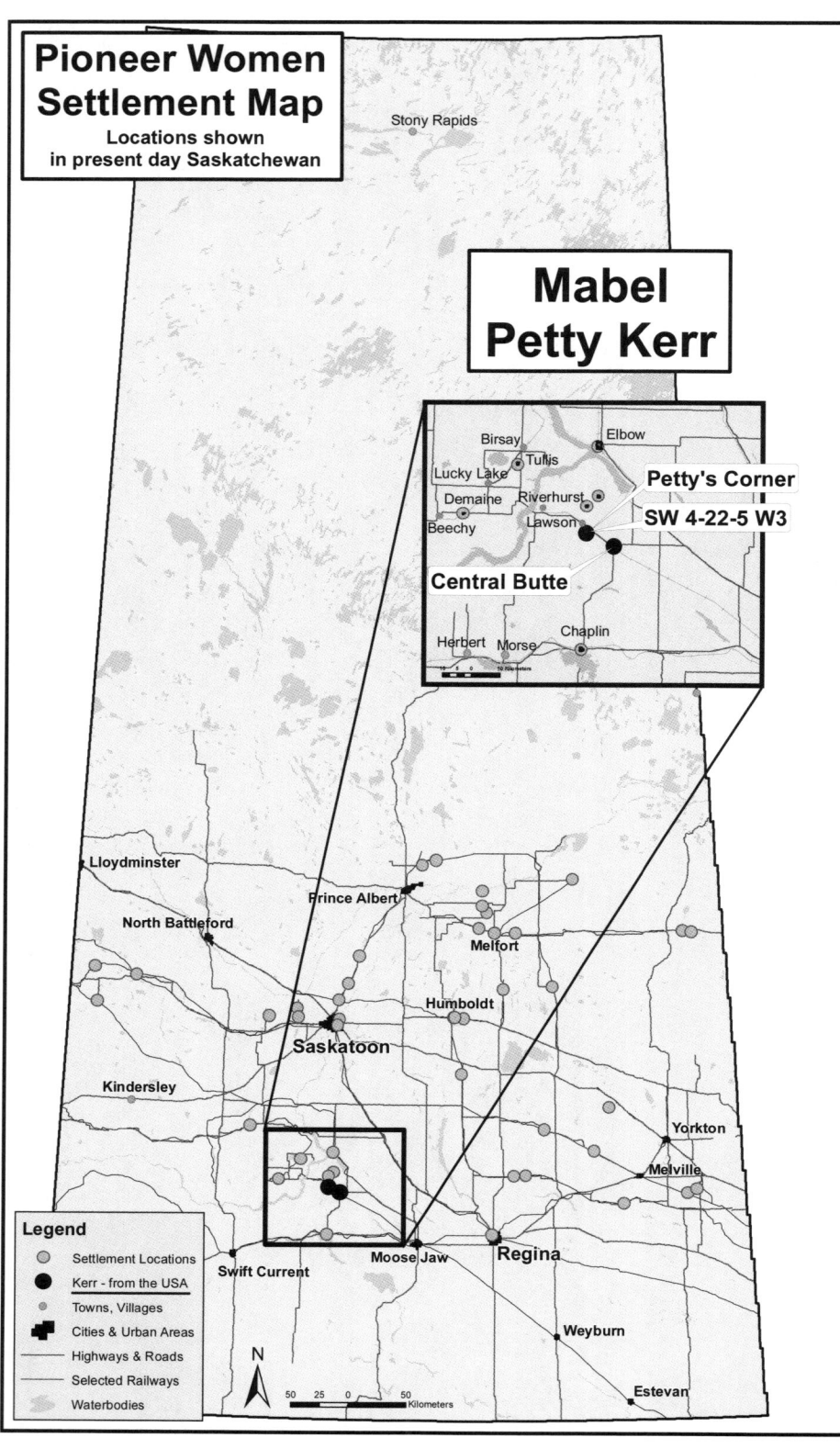

MABEL PETTY KERR
(1895-1981)

Mabel was born on March 16, 1895, in St. Cloud, Minnesota to George and Laura Petty. Mabel's sister Florence was born in 1893 and her sister Eldora in 1901. In May 1906, the entire Petty family moved to Canada to the new province of Saskatchewan, settling about 60 miles west of Moose Jaw. The spot where they homesteaded is still known as Petty's Corner. They ran the post office there until the village of Lawson was established two miles north of the Petty homestead and the post office was moved to Lawson.

In 1906, no schools existed in the area so Mabel and her sisters were taught by their mother who had been a teacher in the U.S.A. Mabel returned to Kimball, Minnesota a few years later to take her Grade 8 classes, staying with an aunt and uncle in the area. She stayed another year before returning to Saskatchewan.

Impatiently awaiting her return was a young homesteader named Scott Kerr, who had moved to Saskatchewan from Ontario with his family in 1906. By 1914, Scott had a partnership in a general store in the new village of Lawson. Scott ran that store for more than 50 years.

On November 11, 1914, Mabel and Scott were married in the Zion Methodist Church manse[16] in Moose Jaw. Mabel was the first bride in the Lawson district. They were given wedding gifts of a crystal fruit bowl, water pitcher and glasses. In 1914, the railroad was extended to the district of Lawson, Central Butte and up to the South Saskatchewan

---

[16] House in which the minister resided, usually attached to or beside the church

Mabel and Scott Kerr and their daughters

River at Riverhurst. This now provided the locals with opportunities to travel to Moose Jaw more easily and the Kerrs could now receive supplies for their store via the train. Before that, supplies had to be brought in by train from Moose Jaw to Chaplin or Bridgeford and then picked up from there by horse and wagon.

The Kerrs lost two children in infancy – John and Marian. They raised two daughters: Arlene (1916), who trained as a registered nurse and then returned to Lawson and married Dave Crowley; and Margery (1921), who became a teacher and met and married Rea Martin while teaching at Herschel, Saskatchewan.

The family lived above the store in Lawson for more than 50 years. To access their home, they had to climb steep wooden steps on the outside of the building. Climbing these steps seemed like they were climbing a mountain – going straight up. At one point when Arlene was about nine years old, she was carrying in a pail of drinking water that she had retrieved from the well two blocks away. As she started to climb the steps up to their home, she lost her footing and stumbled. She saved all the water in the pail but broke her glasses in the process. The stairs were never replaced. Mabel and family as well as their visitors continued to use this treacherous entrance for their home.

Mabel was very active in the community. She was a life member of Lawson United Church Women, life member of Prosperity Rebekah Lodge #81, member of Central Butte Eastern Star Lodge, secretary of Lawson United Church for 45 years and a mainstay in the church's choir. Her dedication to the choir went beyond singing. Every Sunday night, choir practice was held at the Kerrs' residence and Mabel always served a light lunch after the evening rehearsal. This snack usually included buns or sandwiches, cheese, pickles, perhaps some hard-boiled eggs, plus cake, cookies and coffee or tea. In rural Saskatchewan, a lunch was always served to visitors who stopped in between the main meals of breakfast, dinner and supper.

For 25 years, Mabel and four friends played bridge every Thursday afternoon. The hostess prepared supper for the other ladies. Every Christmas, there was a flurry of baking in Mabel's home as she packed cookies and Christmas cake for all the bachelors in the district.

Lawson, like many small towns, revolved around a July 1 sports day in the summer, fowl suppers in the fall and the rink in the winter. Mabel was always baking pies for these events. The town's last sports day was held on July 1, 1963, and Mabel baked for it, too.

Mabel was also a great seamstress, sewing for her daughters and herself. She was like a knitting machine during the war years, turning out hundreds of socks, mitts and balaclavas for service men. She also received some acclaim for knitting unique diamond vests in the early 1950s for all the men in her life – her husband, two sons-in-law and four grandsons. A photo of all the men together wearing their vests was published in the American *McCall's Needlework* magazine. The whole district was very proud of Mabel's accomplishment.

When Lawson School was open in the 1950s and 1960s, Mabel made dinner every school day for her three Crowley grandsons Scott, Lee and Blair during their lunch break. The other grandchildren, Greg and Lynn Martin, grew up on a farm near Herschel. In 1965, Mabel and Scott sold the store and moved to a house in Lawson. This meant no more climbing of the tall steep stairs up to their home above the store. They moved to Central Butte for a few years to be nearer the hospital and doctors because of health concerns.

Mabel died on March 20, 1981, just four days after her 87th birthday. She is buried in the Central Butte Cemetery beside Scott, her husband of over 65 years, and their two infant children.

By Arlene Crowley and Margery Martin, daughters

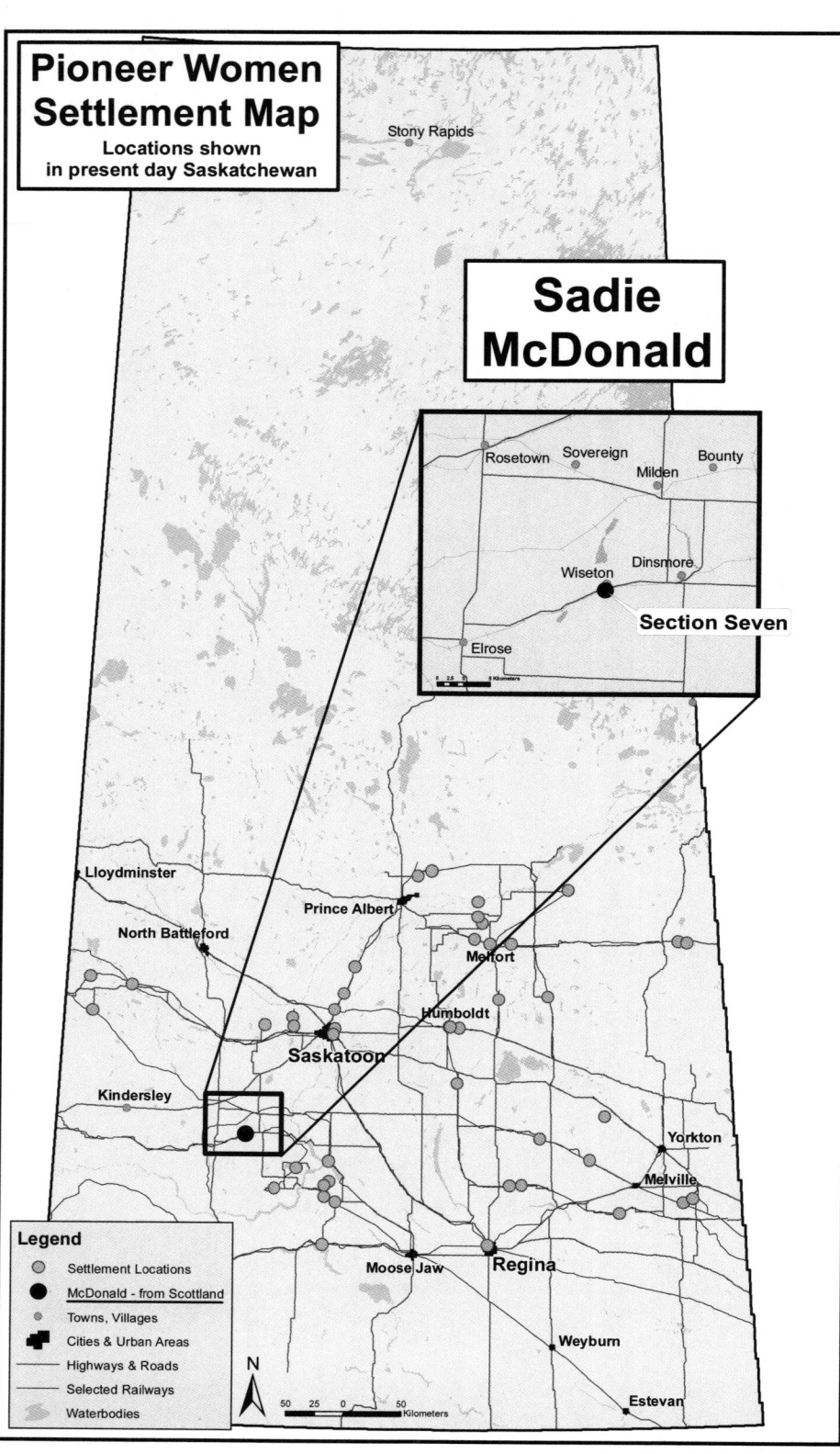

SADIE MCDONALD
(1896-1971)

Sadie was born on April 16, 1896, to Duncan McBeth from Pitlochry, Scotland and Isabel Campbell, who was also of Scottish lineage. Sadie was born in Widdifield, a small community outside of North Bay, Ontario. There, in her log-cabin home, she grew up on her parents' small farm. The house was crowded with sisters and brothers, each doing their share of chores as well as attending school and church. Together, the large family enjoyed evenings of music, singing and dancing.

Sadie's young life was spent not only working at her parents' farm, but helping out neighbouring households when assistance was needed with cooking, childcare and gardening. In those years, farm girls had little training in other fields.

In 1915, Sadie married Edward McDonald, also of Scottish descent, in North Bay, ON. Prior to their marriage, each of them had made a trip west to follow relatives who had settled on homesteads. Both obtained short-term employment. Edward worked for the Canadian Pacific Railway as a brake repairman in Moose Jaw while Sadie spent time in the village of Brownlee as a housekeeper. These jobs were not sustainable and the couple returned to North Bay, where they were married. Their union created an adventurous spirit once more and the newlyweds headed west again, travelling by train to Moose Jaw. Two of Sadie's sisters, Lila Wooden and Maggie Coakwell, had already married farmers and set up homesteads north of Moose Jaw.

The McDonald family: (Back row, left to right) Burns, Helen and Eddie; (Middle row, left to right) Olive, Marnie, Jean, Beth and Fay; (Front row, left to right) Sadie, Jack, Dorothy, Jim and Edward

Sadie's hard work began in her new environment in 1916, when she and Edward took up permanent residency in a small sod house almost eight miles south of Wiseton. Edward had not yet become a true homesteader as he was hired to plow new land with his three oxen by a local farmer. The section of land was not purchased – only rented. In later years, Edward and Sadie made the land purchase. A two-storey home was already on the site. Farm equipment was scarce, simple and labour-intensive. A wagon, plow, tools, two horses, a cow and a few chickens were collected, some of which were donated by neighbouring homesteaders. Growing grain was then, as now, a risky endeavour. Rain, drought, frost, hail, insects, rust, grass fires and high winds were common.

Hardships continued for many years for Sadie. In winter, she melted snow for wash water, carried and chopped wood for the stove, churned cream in quart sealers and made countless pans of soap using tallow and lye. Long days were spent in the kitchen with very few conveniences. Cooking for a hired man and a housekeeper as well as her own family drained enormous amounts of energy from her body. Bedtime couldn't come soon enough. As she wound the alarm clock on a regular basis, she would often request that one of her daughters rub her tired feet. Sadie's stamina was amazing. No duties were shirked, no complaining was ever heard and her working hours were exceedingly long.

Her greatest discomfort and disappointment came when a house fire destroyed the entire home, furnishings, barn, animals and a new Model T car. The sad event took place in 1932 while she was hospitalized in the Elrose Hospital giving birth to her son Burns. The family was housed in a vacant farm home one and a half miles north. They were all extremely grateful for many donations of clothing and household necessities from friends and neighbours. Luckily, the family was able to move into a brand new home 10 months later, just in time for Christmas.

Sadie and Edward's family grew to 13 children over a span of 20 years: Beth (1916), Margaret, Edward, Jean, Dorothy, Duncan, Rae, Helen, Olive, Fay, Burns, Jack and Jim (1936). Two baby boys of the 13 children died in infancy. Most of the children were born at home with the help of a neighbouring midwife. Youngest members of the family were born in Elrose and Milden hospitals – not too far from Wiseton. Older sisters cared lovingly for each new baby, helping with many tasks both inside and outside the home. As siblings grew older, they moved away one by one to pursue new interests.

Sadie was held in high esteem by others. She exemplified patience, resourcefulness, truth and serenity. She was extremely happy when the whole extended family was around her. She was an excellent cook (especially her pies and doughnuts), had a lovely singing voice, a good sense of humour and was a great listener.

Little time was available for hobbies but when possible, Sadie took time to help out at church and in the community. She enjoyed quilting bees held every so often, darned many socks and patched many trousers. She looked forward to the spring months when baby chicks were hatched. Spring housecleaning was almost a delight – her daughters scrubbed, painted and varnished while afternoon tea with cookies was prepared by Sadie. Too little time was set aside for travelling, unfortunately, although a few trips with her husband back to her roots in North Bay were enjoyed. Sadie kept in touch with family members by writing newsy letters, which she enjoyed.

Sadie's grandchildren were very special to her and today, her grandchildren have wonderful memories of Grandma Eddie. They spent time with her playing cards, gathering eggs, cuddling in the rocking chair, eating her special breakfasts while warming their feet on the oven door, making pies and doughnuts, loving her oatmeal cookies and enjoying vacations at the farm. They loved to see her dress up in her best clothes, but especially remember her print housedresses layered with an extra-large apron. Grandma Eddie, to her grandchildren, was a very kind and special grandma and the heart of a loving family.

The beautiful bronze Egg Money statue at the Farmer's Market in Saskatoon captures the physical features of Sadie very well with her strong, tall slim body and her head held high. This elegant woman with children, a cream can and chickens at her feet keeps memories of Sadie alive for her family.

From Widdifield to Wiseton, Sadie's journey through life ended in 1971. Her grave is located at Holt Cemetery, only six miles north and east from the farm. She is at rest, well deserved, and at peace with Grandpa Eddie. It is a beautiful place ... on a small knoll, surrounded by fields of grain blowing in the wind and the beautiful Prairie sunsets complete the picture of the final resting place of Sadie McDonald.

By Helen McDonald-Lewis, daughter

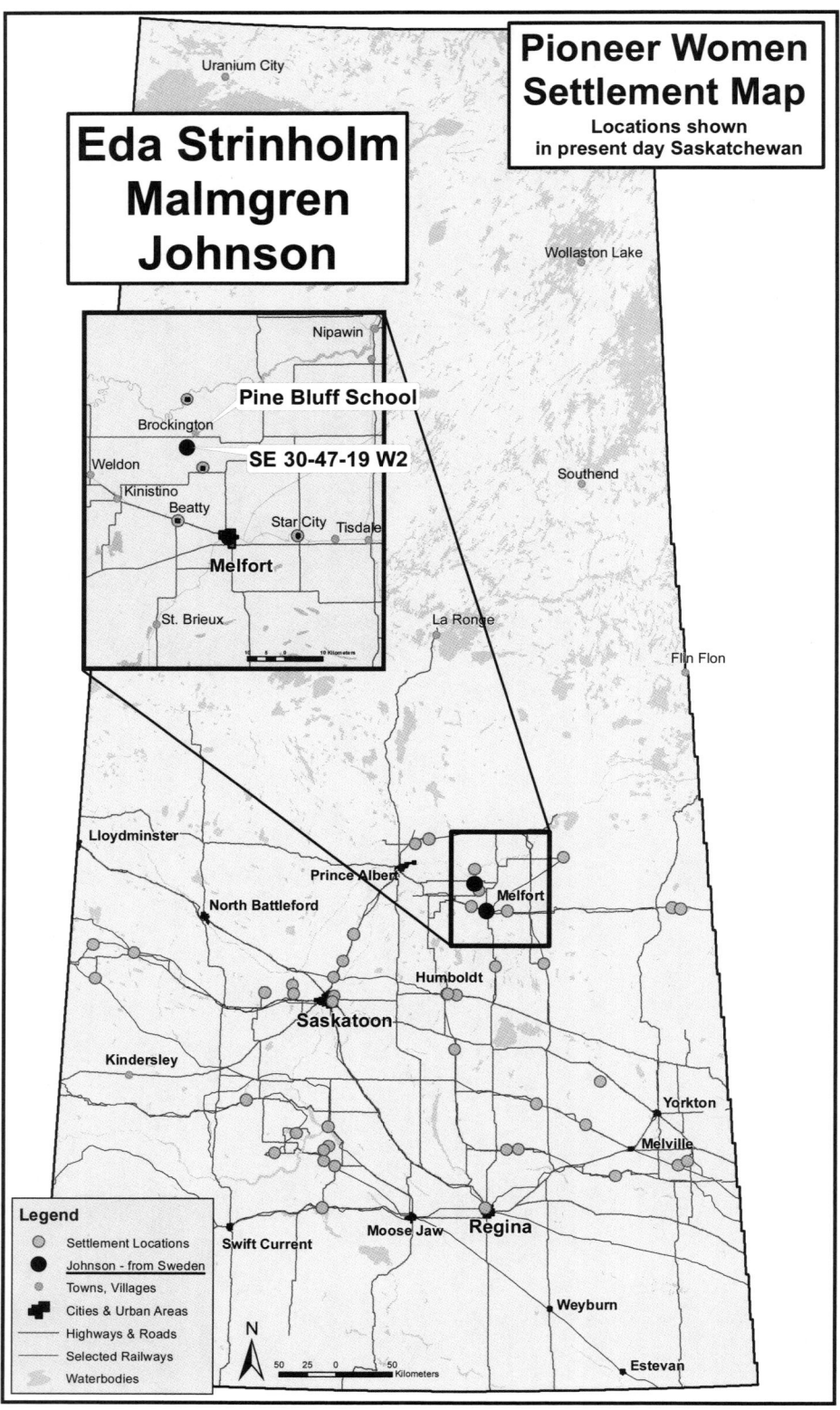

EDA STRINHOLM MALMGREN JOHNSON (1897-1985)

Jenny Eda Maria Strinholm was born on May 18, 1897, in Bredträsk, Bjurholm, Västerbotten, Sweden. The Strinholm family had read in magazines that people in Canada were so prosperous that they had currants in their bread! Many posters in Sweden showed Canadian apple and orange trees and trees with dollar bills on them. Eda's brothers Valentine and Lauren, however, who had immigrated to Canada earlier, had written home to Sweden and told the family how wild it was with bears and wolves. Eda, who had planned to go to Canada earlier and alone at the age of 15 decided, upon receipt of the news of bears and wolves, to wait and go with her older sister.

She travelled to Canada at the age of 16 with her sister Kristina Jacobsson, Kristina's husband August and son Ingemar. The boat docked in Halifax one month after leaving Sweden. They travelled by train directly to Melfort, Saskatchewan in September 1913. Unable to speak English, they had to spend the first night in a horse barn.

Eda went to work for another Swede, Peter From, but soon left to help her brothers with haying. She spent the winter living with her sister Kristina. The next year, she worked for Dick Gunn, who lived 10 miles north of Melfort. She earned $15 per month and worked there for seven months. Once again, she spent the winter with the Jacobssons. In 1915, Eda went to work for Jonas Flodell, a Swedish immigrant. Her job consisted of driving horses, stooking, digging potatoes, cooking and housekeeping. It was during the summer of 1915 that she met Olof Malmgren.

Eda and Olof Malmgren with Eaner and Edner

Olof Artur Malmgren was born on November 18, 1883, in Skivsjön, North Degerfors, Västerbotten, Sweden. He and his brother Jonas Nordstrom immigrated to Canada in 1905. Their brother, Eric Carlson, had immigrated to Canada a year earlier. After arriving in Melfort, they worked on the Canadian Pacific Railway bridge east of Kinistino. In the fall of 1905, the three brothers decided to file for homesteads. They walked the Settler's Trail from Melfort to Prince Albert to file their claims.

When they returned from Prince Albert, they followed cutlines[17] made by survey crews to locate their new homesteads. Sometimes big sloughs took them miles out of their way. In one case, they walked through water up to their necks.

In the winter of 1906, when the three brothers were working at a logging camp, a tree top fell on Olof. He was hit

---

[17] A line cut through the bush; e.g. as a survey line

on the head and chest and knocked to the ground where he lay unconscious in a pool of blood. His ribs were fractured and his lungs punctured. It took one week for Olof to regain consciousness. The camp foreman, Tom Campbell, witnessed the accident and was amazed that Olof survived. Campbell said that the three brothers were the toughest and best men he had ever hired in his 40 years as foreman and that after having them work for him, he always looked for a man who was a 'Swede' and who could spit his tobacco against the wind! Olof never really fully recovered from that accident. He always coughed and had frequent chest pains.

Olof and Eda married on December 6, 1915. Eda was 18 and Olof was 33. They moved into Olof's one-room log house that had an upstairs which Olof and his brother Jonas built in 1905. An addition was built onto the house to create a total of four rooms. Eda and Olof had seven children: Edner (1916), Eaner, Nannie, Margaret, Alf, Doreen and Elvin (1928).

The Malmgren children were gifted musicians and singers. Elvin and Alf and all three girls played the guitar and sang. Eaner played the mouth organ. Neighbours visited often, bringing a guitar and violin to sing and play along with the Malmgren family.

In 1930, the crops were snowed in. Olof, Edner and Eaner were threshing while Eda and Nannie were shaking snow off the bundles. Olof caught a chill shovelling grain and developed double pneumonia. He passed away on November 22, 1930.

The family suffered many hardships after Olof's death. The workload fell on Eda and the older children. A neighbour occasionally helped with difficult tasks on the farm. Eda asked her boys to take homemade bread and milk to the neighbour as a partial payment for the work he had done. On one occasion, she sewed the neighbour an elk-hide jacket, complete with beading on the front and back.

Eda often went to Pine Bluff School to get second-hand clothes that were provided by a relief organization. She made her own patterns, cut down the coats and made new ones for her children. She also made dresses, blouses and shirts and was very proud that her children looked so smart. She knitted mitts, socks and hats for all her children and later for her many grandchildren. Old clothing was also cut into strips that were woven into mats on a loom for scatter rugs in the house.

Eda married Oscar Johnson, a local farmer, in Melfort and moved to the Johnson farm 10 miles away. Oscar's first wife had passed away, leaving him with their five children. The eldest was 14 and the youngest was less than two years old when Eda and Oscar's son Gerald was born in 1939. Eda now had another young family to raise.

All the farming was done with horses until 1939 when a Cockshutt 70 tractor was purchased. Eda worked hard on the farm, milking cows daily and shipping cream to the creamery in Melfort every week. She also made butter. The chicken coop was filled with laying hens and Eda sold the eggs for extra money. Her favourite part of this venture was serving coffee to everyone who came to buy the eggs! Roosters were raised for butchering in the fall and many family members received these birds, which were often the size of small turkeys!

Eda and her daughters got together during summer months to make large batches of Swedish thin bread on a wood stove in a granary. Eda also had quite a green thumb. The sunroom attached to the main house had many geraniums that she loved to tend. Her large garden was always planted with 800 to 900 hills of potatoes and many five-gallon pails of potatoes were carried out and stored for the winter.

Most minor injuries were dealt with on the farm with homemade remedies. Eda routinely had terrible nose bleeds and had to make the long journey to Melfort to have the blood vessels cauterized.

Eda never did speak fluent English and often mixed Swedish and English together. For example, instead of saying roosters, she said "tuppa." The word island became "is land."

Oscar passed away in 1975. Gerald took over the family farm and Eda moved into a small house in the farmyard. She lived in that house until a few weeks before her death on September 5, 1985.

Eda is buried beside her first husband Olof Malmgren at the Brockington Mission Covenant Church Cemetery in the North Star district northwest of Melfort.

By Dale Malmgren, grandson (Edner's son)

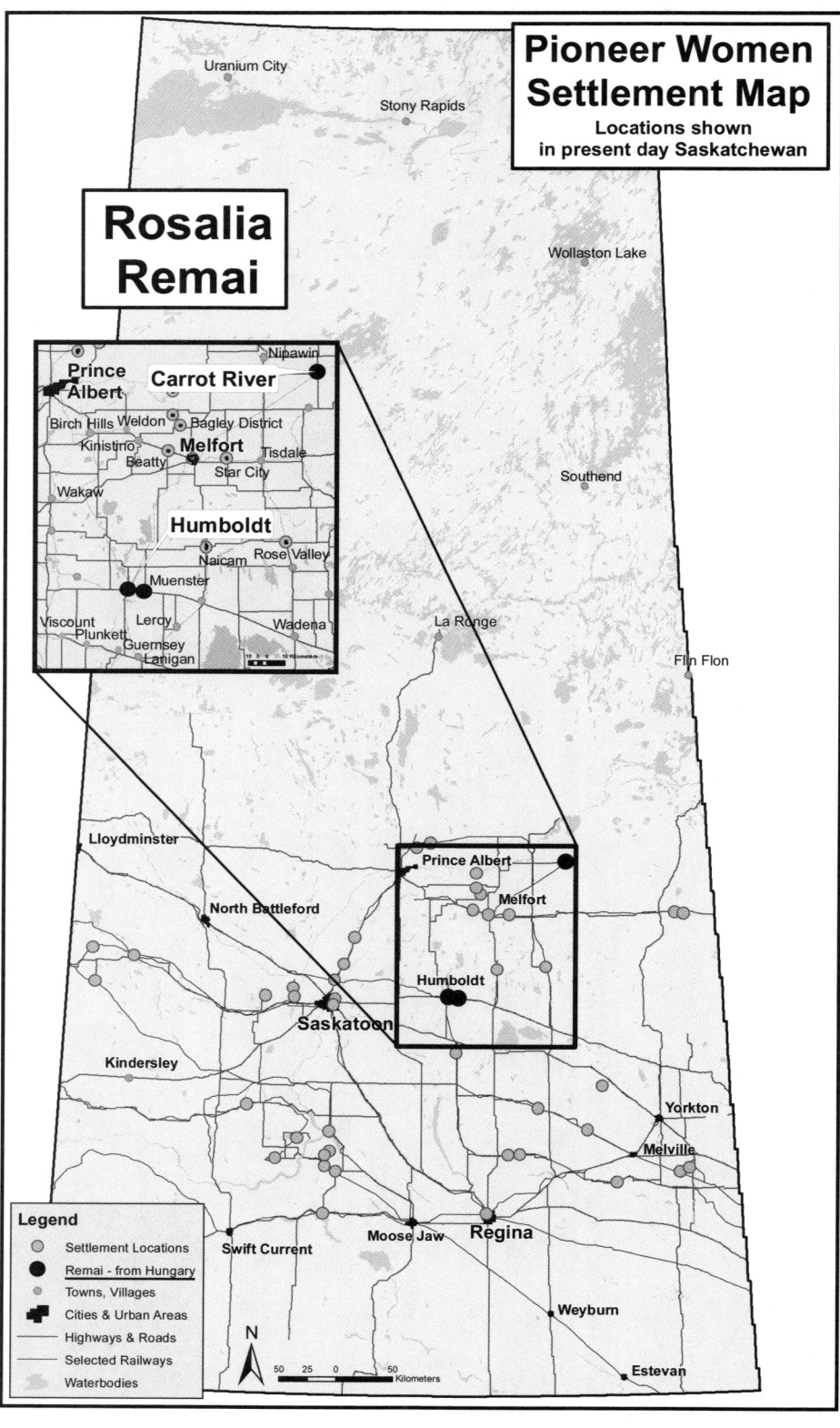

ROSALIA REMAI
(1898-1971)

Rosalia was born Rosalia Remai in Bakonysarkany, Hungary in 1898. She married Steve Remai (no relation) in Hungary in 1922. She and Steve had several children by the time Steve immigrated to Canada in 1926. A year later, Rosalia and the children began the long trip to Canada.

They travelled by train to the port of Cherbourg, France where on May 6, 1927, they boarded the ship Ascania, arriving in Canada on May 16, 1927, at the port in Quebec City. From there they travelled by train to Humboldt, Saskatchewan where Rosalia was reunited with her husband. She brought many household items with her such as dishes, cookware, linen and bedding as well as family mementoes from Hungary. Rosalia spoke no English or French. One can only imagine the trials and tribulations she must have encountered along the way.

In the following years, the family lived in various areas of the province including Muenster, Plunkett, Guernsey and Leroy. Fortunately, in some of these places there were other families who spoke Hungarian, which encouraged an occasional social get-together on a Sunday.

Farm life was very difficult and Rosalia was very involved with the labours of farming. In addition to helping look after livestock and poultry, Rosalia planted a huge garden to provide fresh vegetables for her growing family and for canning purposes. It was a difficult time to establish a successful farm in these areas. To supplement the meagre farm income, her husband had to find employment on road projects

Rosalia Remai

or on other farms. During these times Rosalia managed the farm with the help of her children. All farming was done with horses. Farm wells had no pumps so water was pulled up with a pail and rope or, in some cases, a pulley system.

During the 'Dirty Thirties' the family encountered many farming difficulties. They had to contend with grasshoppers, hail, late spring frosts, early fall frosts, drought and dust storms which invaded even the most air-tight homes. Having been devastated by these problems, the family decided to move to the Carrot River area in the spring of 1942. Rosalia and Steve had purchased a quarter section of land for the grand sum of $500 cash plus 4,826 bushels of wheat. The family travelled by train to Carrot River along with all their household items, machinery and livestock. From there, Steve and the older boys herded the livestock to the new farm five miles east of Carrot River. The rest of the family walked or rode on the wagons carrying all of the household contents. The machinery was pulled by teams of horses. By the time this move took place, the family consisted of Rosalia and Steve plus 10 children ranging in age from three to 18. The oldest daughter was raised by her grandparents in Hungary.

Their first home at Carrot River was rather small for a family of 12. On a cold morning, it wasn't unusual to have a thin layer of ice on top of the water pail. However, under Rosalia's guidance the family managed quite well. In the warmer months the boys moved into an empty granary to give everyone more room.

By growing a large garden, Rosalia canned peas and mustard beans. Dill pickles were made in huge crocks and every fall, she harvested enough cabbage to shred into a large barrel for sauerkraut. The sauerkraut was a favourite served with the farm-raised pork ribs. Rosalia also made large rounds of cheddar cheese, prepared cottage cheese, churned her own butter and made sour cream and whipping cream. The family's large herd of cows provided the milk to create all these homemade dairy products. All milking was done by hand and completed before breakfast. While the milking and separating was being done, Rosalia was busy preparing breakfast and lunches for the children going to school.

As well as using the milk for family foods, Rosalia and Steve shipped cream to the local dairy. She churned butter that was carefully stamped with a butter print and also sold eggs, turkeys and chickens. The money from these sales was used to purchase things that could not be produced on the farm – staples such as sugar, salt, yeast, flour and coffee.

To feed her large family, Rosalia baked bread regularly. She started the yeast in the evening and made the dough very early the next morning. By the time the family woke, she had 12 or 14 loaves of freshly baked bread ready. To add to their food supply, bacons and hams were smoked and sausages were made. Occasionally, a rabbit or prairie chicken was shot.

Every fall during threshing time, the neighbours pitched in to help each other. There were usually an extra eight to 10 people for Rosalia to feed, including the morning and afternoon coffee breaks and lunches. Some of the wheat and oats harvested were taken to the flourmill in Humboldt to be made into oatmeal for breakfast, flour for baking or Red River cereal.

The Carrot River area was lush with wild berries such as

saskatoons, blueberries, raspberries and strawberries. The children picked the berries and Rosalia made all kinds of jams, jellies, syrups and canned fruit. She even incorporated many of these berries into her baking. Even today, her children reminisce about the wonderful canned fruit and other preserves they enjoyed during the long winter months.

Rosalia had a treadle sewing machine that she used for making dresses for herself and her girls. She taught her daughters how to embroider on pillowcases and aprons made from bleached flour sacks. Sheets were also made from flour sacks. Rosalia washed and carded sheep wool and spun it into yarn and also taught her children to knit socks and mitts. In the winter evenings, she darned socks, sewed on missing buttons and patched clothes by lamplight after the children had finished their homework and were tucked into bed. Often at night, she did some laundry to hang outside on the clothesline early in the morning. Dirty clothes were washed on a scrub board and ironing was done with flat irons heated on the stove. In later years, she used a washing machine that had to be rocked back and forth and had a wringer that was operated by hand.

Entertainment was very limited for Rosalia and Steve and their family. The parents made sure their religious training wasn't neglected. Every summer the children walked into town for a one-week course based on the Baltimore Catechism. Sunday mornings were hectic for Rosalia. Besides the regular morning tasks, the family had to be readied for Sunday mass. The children were dressed in their finest. The family went to church by horse and buggy or caboose in winter. In the evenings on the weekend, the children sat around the wood stove and Steve read the Hungarian newspaper to them. It usually contained a story that continued from month to month. A radio with a battery pack was reserved for listening to music on Sunday and the occasional newscast.

The Christmas season was a special time for the Remai family. Steve brought home a big Christmas tree and Rosalia made popcorn to string together to decorate the tree. She also made small sugar cookies and a special Hungarian lattice cake. A small Christmas gift, often home-made, was placed under the tree for each person in the family. Once the tree was decorated, the children gathered around to pray and were sent off to bed. The next day, a Christmas turkey dinner was made with farm-grown turkey, vegetables and Rosalia's baking.

Times continued to get better and their hard work began to pay off. The Remai family moved into a new house in 1950. This house featured four bedrooms, a bathroom, utility room, a porch, a large kitchen, living room and a full basement with a wood and coal furnace. It also had a well in the basement with a pump bringing water to the kitchen sink It was a very important gathering centre for the family for many years because to Rosalia, "family was everything." A new barn was built in 1953 with the construction efforts being led by their son John, who was a newly certified journeyman carpenter.

Rosalia left many fond memories for the family to cherish. She was a pioneer woman in the truest sense of the word. She endured and survived many hardships so she and her husband Steve could provide a better life for their family. Rosalia passed away on December 23, 1971. She was laid to rest in the local cemetery in Carrot River.

By Mary Fox, daughter

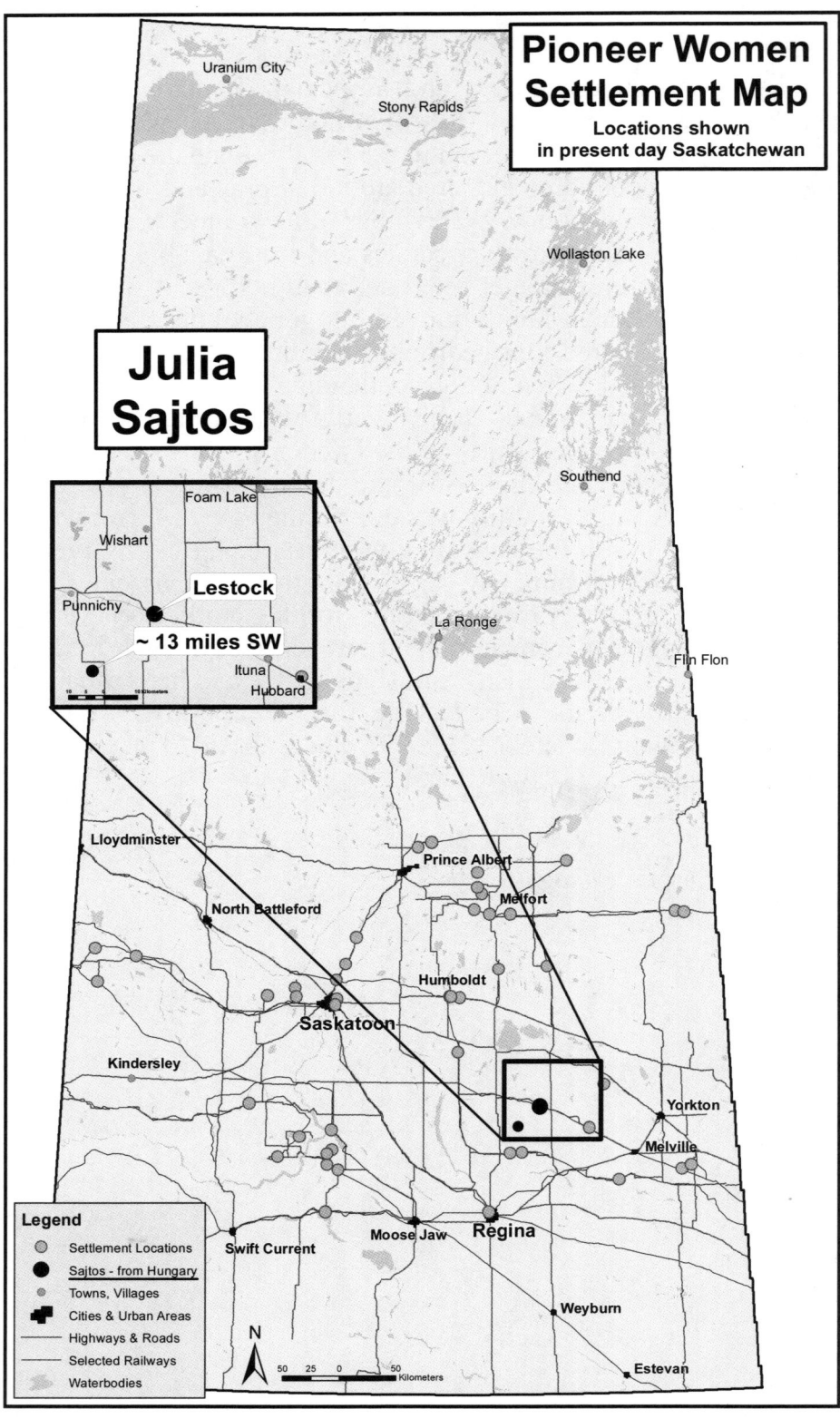

JULIA SAJTOS
(1903-1971)

Julia was born on November 12, 1903, to Benjamin and Sophie Sajtos in Hungary. She was the oldest of six siblings.

She married Louis Sajtos (no relation) on January 31, 1922, in Mandok, Hungary. She gave birth to two children before her husband left Hungary in 1926 to seek a better life in Canada, following the lure of owning 160 acres of homestead land.

Louis acquired a homestead 13 miles southwest of Lestock, Saskatchewan and worked for two years to save enough money to be able to pay the fare for his wife and children. In December 1928, with her five-year-old daughter and two-year-old son, Julia sailed across the Atlantic on the ship Pennland. They spent Christmas on the ship and arrived at Pier 21 in Halifax on December 28, but because her son was sick when they arrived in Canada, they were put in quarantine for several days. After being released, they took the train to Lestock, Saskatchewan where Louis was awaiting their arrival.

When Julia and the children arrived in Canada, the family lived with friends during the first winter until Louis built the home in which they lived until their retirement. Over the years, the house was added onto but the original structure always remained.

Between 1929 and 1940, Julia gave birth to four more children – two girls and two boys.

Life on the farm was one of hard work but the family always had enough to eat. Julia made fresh-baked bread,

Julia Sajtos

which tasted wonderful with homemade butter and jelly. She made jelly from wild berries such as strawberries, raspberries, saskatoons and chokecherries. Picking berries was a fun time. In a sense, it was an escape from having to do work, and there was always something waiting to be done on the farm. Julia grew rhubarb and red currants in her garden from which she also made jelly. She also canned the wild strawberries, raspberries and saskatoons and stored them in the cellar of the house. This made for great desserts in the cold winter. The family ate chicken, beef and pork that was raised on the farm. In some cases wild meat was acquired by hunting – namely deer, ducks and prairie chickens.

Julia kept a huge garden, milked cows and assisted with all aspects of farm work. And yes, the eggs. This was a daily ritual: gathering the eggs, cleaning and buffing them, having them ready to take to town once a week. It was with this egg money that she bought the necessary groceries: flour, salt, sugar, rice and some fresh fruit. Her children anxiously awaited her return from town because she always made sure they each received a treat. To this day, Cracker Jack popcorn evokes many fond childhood memories for her offspring. This was especially fascinating because Julia had only a limited command of the English language.

Julia loved to do handiwork, but with all the work on the farm and doing the sewing and mending for the family, she only had limited time for hobbies. The family belonged to the United Church and a Hungarian minister from Winnipeg made four or five trips a year during the spring/summer/autumn months. Close to the farm was a small church where services were held. Julia always saw to it that the church was cleaned and ready for the service. She also brought the bread for Holy Communion.

Julia's children often marvelled at how their mother, coming to a foreign land, not being able to speak the language, had the fortitude to adapt and raise six children with sheer hard work.

The family lived on the homestead until Julia and Louis retired into the village of Lestock in 1961. Julia was rarely sick throughout her life. She was always there when her children arrived home from school and later, when they came home from college for a visit. Even after the children were married, Julia was waiting with a hot meal ready for them and their families. Because of her constant presence and support, it was a great shock to all when Julia died of a heart attack in May 1971 at the age of 67. Louis died in 1974.

Julia and Louis always longed to return to Hungary, but they never made it back. No other siblings of Julia or Louis moved to Canada. Consequently, their family had no aunts, uncles or cousins living in Canada. Julia's youngest brother made a visit to Canada but unfortunately, it was after both Julia and Louis had passed away. Several of Julia's children and grandchildren have made visits to Hungary and met some of their relatives.

Both Julia and Louis are buried in the cemetery at Lestock.

By Vi Hultin, daughter

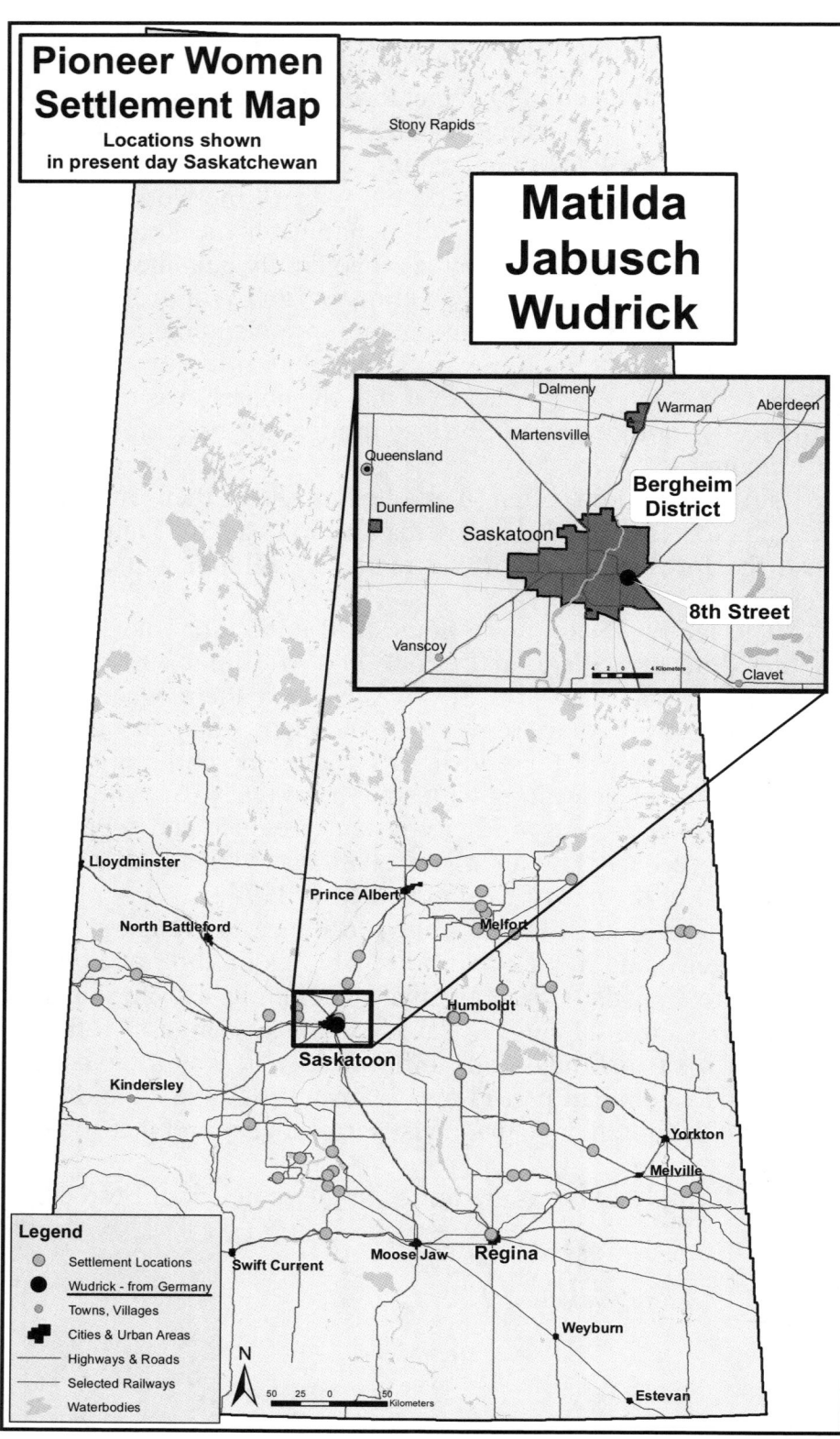

MATILDA JABUSCH WUDRICK
(1905-1987)

Matilda was born in Beausejour, Manitoba in June 1905, and would become the eldest of 11 children. Her parents were Bertha Adolf, born in Gelsendorf, Germany who emigrated with her widowed mother to the Rosenfeld area of Manitoba in the late 1880s and August Jabusch, born in 1878 in Niezpodzanka III, Volhynia, Poland. His family also settled in the Rosenfeld area at that time.

Matilda became a city girl when her father went to work for the railroad in Winnipeg and her mother set up a boarding house for railroaders. She even took piano lessons until her father caught the land hunger that so many European immigrants brought with them, yearning for a new and better life. He moved his family to a piece of rich farmland in Saskatchewan somewhere near where 8th Street East now runs in Saskatoon.

Despite that good piece of land, August soon resettled the family in the largely German-speaking district of Bergheim (home in the hills) a few miles east of Saskatoon. "Amongst all those stones to pick to get yourself a field" was how his daughter described it in later years.

In 1925, Matilda married Reinhold Wudrick (born Wattrick/Wottrich in Berestowitz, Rowna, Volhynia, Poland) and they settled near their respective families in that same farming district.

Hers was not an easy life. It was full of hard work, poor land and the Dirty Thirties. Matilda worked equally as hard outdoors as she did in the house, much like a horizontal yo-yo:

Matilda Jabusch Wudrick at age 80 with her roses

to the garden, to the babies, milking, hoeing, sewing, cooking, carrying bucket after bucket of water, drawn from the well by rope, to do laundry, canning, cooking again, and working to keep both house and family scrubbed up "within an inch."

She knew when the cows would calve and she sat in the barn while the sow produced her babies. Matilda once brought the runt of a pig's litter into the house wrapped in an old towel. She set it on the open oven door in hopes that a little warmth would help the creature survive if she could get enough cow's milk down its scrawny neck. It worked.

More than once, she hovered over dozens of fluffy yellow chicks purchased at the feed store each spring, only to have the weather turn cold again. This meant firing up the little brooder's coal-oil heater that required almost constant attention, then finding out the next morning that many of the chicks hadn't survived the night anyway.

How many times did she cry in sheer desperation? How many migraine headaches did she endure in silence? Only once did she cry in front of her children – when her favourite mare succumbed to milk fever before her very eyes.

Matilda nursed her children through bouts of measles, scarlet fever, mumps and simple colds using homemade cures or good old Watkins camphor ointment.

She was not much of a visitor. If she could be coaxed to visit one of her children's homes after they had grown and were producing children of their own, she made it clear that "it's only for awhile."

She built a reputation as a talented seamstress in the little town of Sutherland, now a part of Saskatoon. The family moved from the farm into Sutherland when the eldest reached high-school age. Matilda could never be too far away from the whirring of that alternative egg money spinner. Not only that, once her youngest became a 'working guy', Matilda herself became an out-of-the-house 'working girl' as a seamstress in a ladies' wear shop in Saskatoon. She loved that life!

Matilda and Reinhold eventually retired to the more kindly West Coast where she spent her later years growing gorgeous roses and puttering in the garden. She died and was buried in Kelowna, B.C. in 1987.

In early 2012, her six children were – perhaps due to those hardy European farming genes – all alive and "pretty well, considering." They all live in Canada, the land their parents' parents chose to make their own: Anne (Wudrick) Morrison and Edward William Wudrick in Kelowna, B.C.; Gordon George Wudrick in Vancouver, B.C.; Lloyd Leslie Wudrick in Saskatoon, Elsie (Wudrick) Davidson and Gertrude (Wudrick) Story in Regina.

One of Matilda's sons said of his efficient and "with-it" mother: "If she'd been born into a different time and circumstance, she could have run a small corporation."

In a way, we might consider that the corporation given to her as her lot in life has grown to encompass not only her six children and their families, but also in turn, their offspring and their extended families – who remember her with much appreciation and with total affection.

By Gertrude Story, daughter

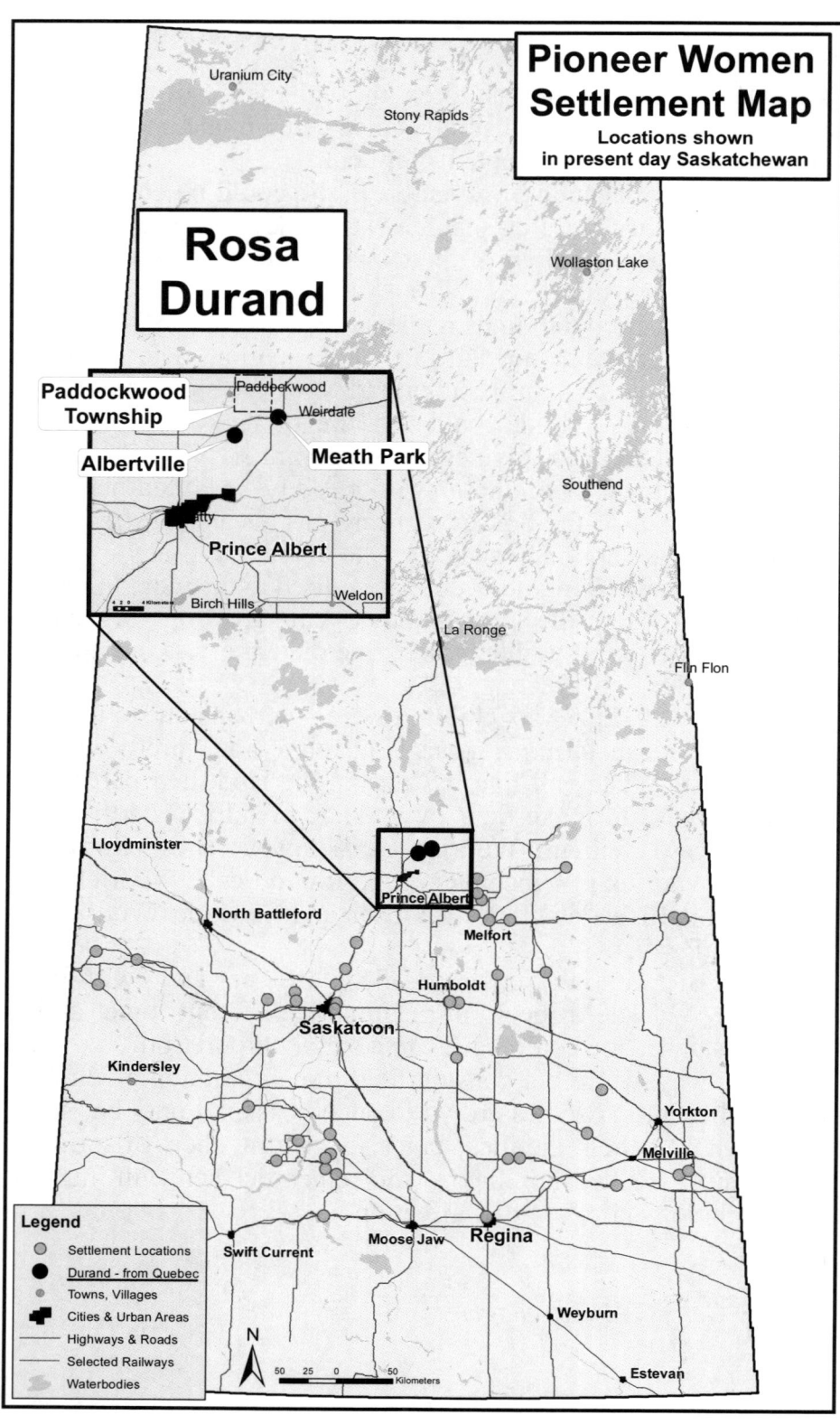

ROSA DURAND
(1906-1997)

Rosa Camire was born on August 15, 1906, in Plessisville, Quebec to Alphonine Dubois and Adlard Camire.

In search of opportunities and a better life, Rosa's family moved with their horse by train to a homestead near Albertville, Saskatchewan where they lived in a one-room log shack. Land was cleared with a horse and plow, and gardens were seeded. Rosa's father made a living by clearing lands for other pioneers.

Three years after their arrival in Albertville, Rosa's mother died from appendicitis. Two years after her mother's death, Rosa's father died from internal bleeding from an injury sustained on the family farm. Rosa was nine and her younger siblings were seven, five and two years old. The older siblings, ages 17 and 15, looked after the younger ones. Life was very difficult with precious little to live on, but somehow they were able to survive.

In February 1924, 17-year-old Rosa married Albany Durand, a local farmer. Rosa moved in with her new husband and his parents Frank and Mary on the parents' homestead four miles northwest of Meath Park in the local home improvement district of Paddockwood Range 24 Township 52. Albany later purchased a 160-acre homestead of his own nearby at a cost of $10. For many years after that, Rosa and Albany cleared the bush off the land so they could plant gardens and raise horses, cattle, hogs, turkeys and chickens to provide for their growing family. Rosa and Albany had eight children: Armand (1925), Alfred, Adelene, Denise, Ellen,

Rosa Durand

Philip, Juliette and Lorraine (1945). Rosa's first two children were born at home under challenging conditions with no midwife. When Rosa's sixth child was born, Rosa almost died from a severe condition called milk legs, a painful swelling of the legs and breasts caused by clots in the veins. As a result, both her breasts were removed. She was hospitalized for two months. This was only one of many serious illnesses she endured.

The work was hard and never-ending. Albany hunted for deer, elk and moose, which provided for most of the family's meat requirements. Rosa canned almost all of the meats and all vegetables from her garden. She also canned berries such as strawberries, raspberries, saskatoons and blueberries. With the berries, she made pies and other desserts. All this canning, cooking and breadmaking was done on a wood-burning stove.

The family did not have electricity until 1955. In the 40 years they were on the farm, the Durands never had a telephone, running water or an indoor washroom. Water was hand-pumped in from a well under the house. Rainwater from eavestroughs was collected into a cistern that was also under the house. This water was used for bathing and laundry. Used water was poured into a sink that drained outside the house to a draining ditch. Later, Rosa had a washing machine that had to be rocked back and forth with a handle. The freshly washed laundry was put through a hand-turned wringer, dropped into a tub of rinsing water and put back through the wringer again. All the clothing was then hung outside on a clothesline to dry. In the winter, the clothes froze, which gave them a clean fresh smell. The house was heated with a buck stove[18]; many times the stove would turn red from overheating. The windows had a layer of frost on them so thick that one could not see outside nor could it be scraped off until spring thaw.

Rosa used a peddle sewing machine to make most of the clothing for herself and the children. She also sewed her own sheets and pillowcases made from bleached flour bags. Rosa often embroidered on the flour bags to make the bedding look prettier. She knit socks, toques, mitts, sweaters and scarves to keep her children warm when they went to school by horse and toboggan in the winter.

Life on the Prairies was very difficult in all the years that Rosa and Albany farmed. Their faith was tested time and time again with droughts, early frost, grasshopper infestations and hailstorms that destroyed the crops, farm buildings and killed animals.

In 1965, Rosa and Albany sold three of their quarter sections of land. With the sale of that land and machinery, they bought an 18-suite apartment building in Prince Albert, which they owned and managed. In 1982, they fully retired and bought a condo in Saskatoon. Finally, life was not as demanding and Rosa could enjoy the fruits of her labour.

Rosa faced incredible obstacles as a pioneer woman but with courage and inner strength, she found ways to overcome her daily hardships and make an imprint on her

---

[18] A wood-fired stove for cooking and heating

community and province. She often said, "We did what we had to do to survive."

Rosa passed away at City Hospital in Saskatoon on January 22, 1997, at the age of 90 and is buried next to her husband Albany at Hillcrest Memorial Gardens in Saskatoon.

By Ellen Remai, daughter

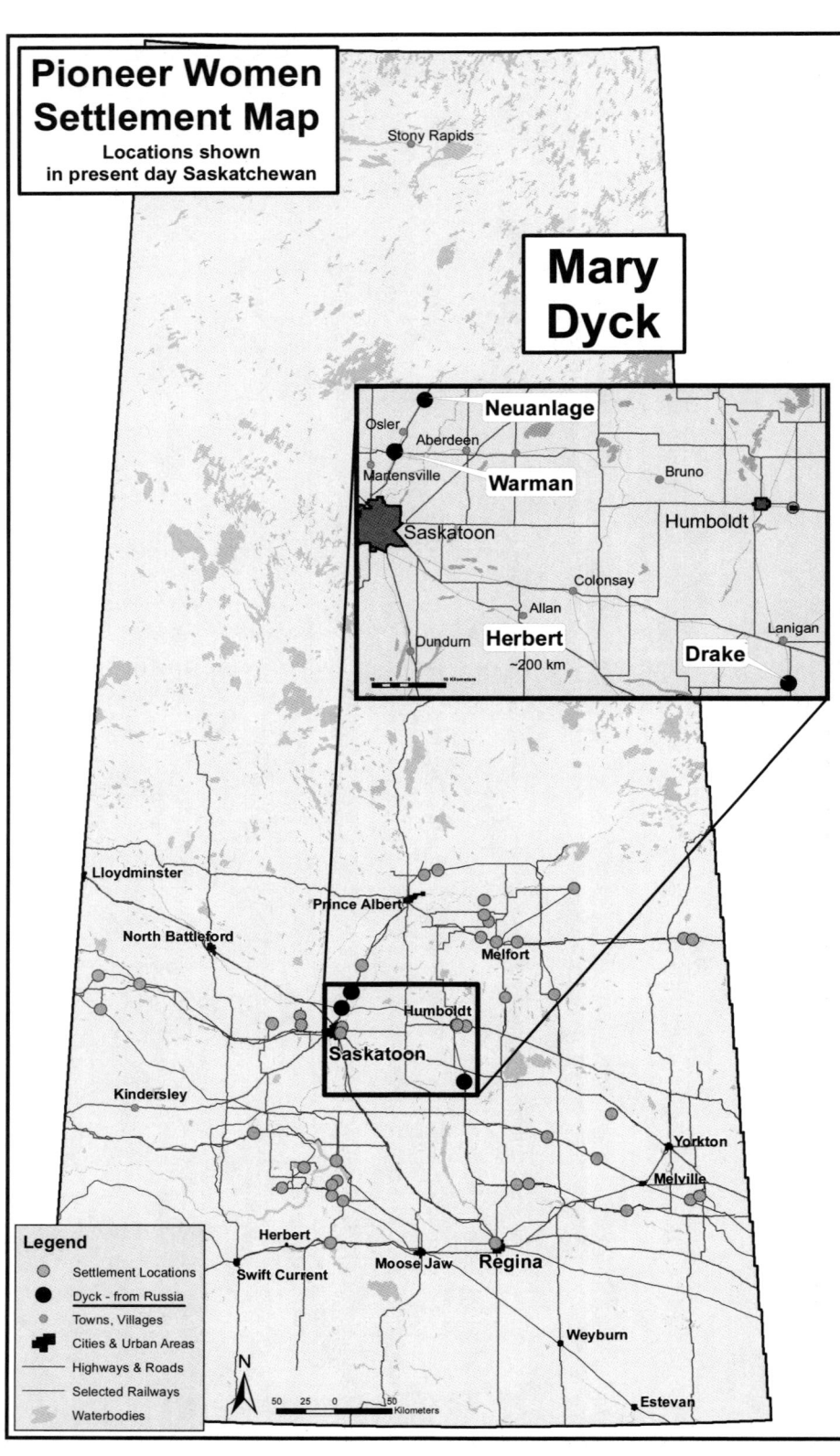

Mary Dyck
(1912-1980)

Mary was born in Nicolaipol, Russia on February 7, 1912. She was the third youngest in a family of 12 children. Personal loss was her constant companion. Both her parents died in 1918, by the time she had her seventh birthday. After her parents died, her family faced severe economic hardship and her older brothers and sisters could not provide for her. Mary, as well as one sister and one brother, was given up for adoption. One of her brothers was conscripted to the Russian army, never to be seen again.

At the age of seven, with nothing but her clothes and her doll, Mary joined the family of Herman Bueckerts as a foster daughter. The family brought her to Canada in 1925 to a new country, a different language and strange customs. She felt alone and afraid.

The Bueckerts met friends in Herbert, Saskatchewan and later moved to Neuanlage near Hague, Saskatchewan. Opportunities for formal education were limited for Mary because her help was needed on the farm. She met Jacob Dyck when they were both baptized and became members of the same church. They were married on November 3, 1934. They farmed at Neuanlage for one year, moved to Drake for a few months, then settled on a farm near Warman.

Mary lost contact with her biological brothers and sisters for some time after she was adopted but in the early years in Canada, she reconnected with some of them. One of her brothers and two of her sisters came to Canada and settled in another region of Saskatchewan. The families then kept in touch.

Mary Dyck and daughter Linda

Between 1938 and 1950, six children – Linda, Alma, Elvin, Abram, Mary Ann and Samuel – were born to Jacob and Mary. Abram and Mary Ann died in infancy.

Mary's pioneering spirit was more than evident with her efforts in agriculture. She contributed to daily life on a mixed farm in a number of ways. Though small in stature, she displayed a strong work ethic, usually being the first family member to start the day with chores of milking cows before preparing breakfast for everyone. Summertime labour consisted of managing a large vegetable garden to offset the cost of groceries. A large fruit tree garden provided plums, gooseberries, raspberries, cherries, rhubarb and currants that were canned for future use. With natural rainfall the only source of water, the quantity of produce varied with weather conditions.

Aside from livestock as a meat supply, chickens were providing the next generation of fowl. This produced a very hardy product as well as meat and eggs throughout the year. If any farm products were in an oversupply, they were bartered, swapped or exchanged with neighbours for the betterment of the community. The storekeeper in Warman often exchanged fresh eggs and butchered chickens for staples such as sugar and flour. One time, Mary traded a pound of butter for a calf!

Autumn brought the task of stooking sheaves in the fields of grain. Early winter brought neighbours together for a hog-butchering bee. Aside from making dinner for the group, Mary assumed the task of preparing the giant feed cooker for the cracklings and spareribs that were ready in early afternoon. This involved starting and keeping the fire at the right temperature, stirring the ingredients until fully cooked and then packaging the meat and lard for storage.

Mary pioneered new ways of doing more with less. Her hobby was embroidery and needlepoint. Many recycled flour sacks, bleached white, were transformed into useful works of art (pillowcases and dresser scarves/runners) to be donated to the Ladies Aid fundraisers or for gifts. Another example of Mary's ingenuity was the many quilts and comforters she created during the long winter months. She was an excellent self-taught seamstress, although most of her talents were directed to mending clothes for her family. A treadle-powered Singer sewing machine performed many tasks, including repairing binder canvas. Whether driven by cruel conditions or just the satisfaction of a job well done, Mary always accepted the challenge.

Mary also helped in construction of buildings. When a log building was scheduled to be turned into a granary, the cracks between the logs needed to be filled so the grain wouldn't spill to the outside. This was accomplished by mixing mud, straw and water in a big tub with her bare feet. This mixture was then plastered onto the walls.

Although hardships were many, there were times set aside for church activities and socializing with neighbours and friends. Mary would contribute with her beautiful singing voice, occasionally accompanied by her husband on the mandolin. She had a keen ability to memorize and deliver German recitations. Her actions served as a role model for her children, who also sang and mastered musical instruments.

Weather dictated much of Mary's life. One particular winter in the 1940s, Jacob took Mary and two of their preschool children to Warman where she boarded the train for a trip to Hague to visit her foster parents. The morning started out clear and sunny. The oldest child went to school but came home early when a weather warning was issued. Chores were done early. Jacob and the daughter fed the livestock and brought wood, coal and water into the house. Then they hitched the team of horses to the caboose to go back to Warman to pick up Mary. By this time, the storm was so severe that the horses refused to cross the railroad tracks in Warman to get to the railroad station. Jacob and the oldest daughter stayed in town at a service station due to the storm and were unaware that Mary and the children were staying overnight at the Warman hotel. The family was reunited in the morning.

While admired for her work, Mary will be remembered for her love. She was strong in character yet gentle in spirit. She desired a brighter future for her children than what she had experienced and she instilled in them her love of learning, always encouraging them to do their best in school. She made personal sacrifices for the overall well-being of the family. During family disputes, she was the glue that held the family together, at times with nothing more than her unshakeable personal faith in God to keep her going.

Mary and Jacob retired and moved to Warman in 1977. Mary passed away on April 6, 1980. She is buried in the Osler Cemetery.

The word pioneer can be used as a noun, a verb and as an adjective. Each of these describes Mary Dyck.

Mary Dyck. A pioneer of action. A pioneer in belief. A pioneering spirit.

By the family of Mary Dyck

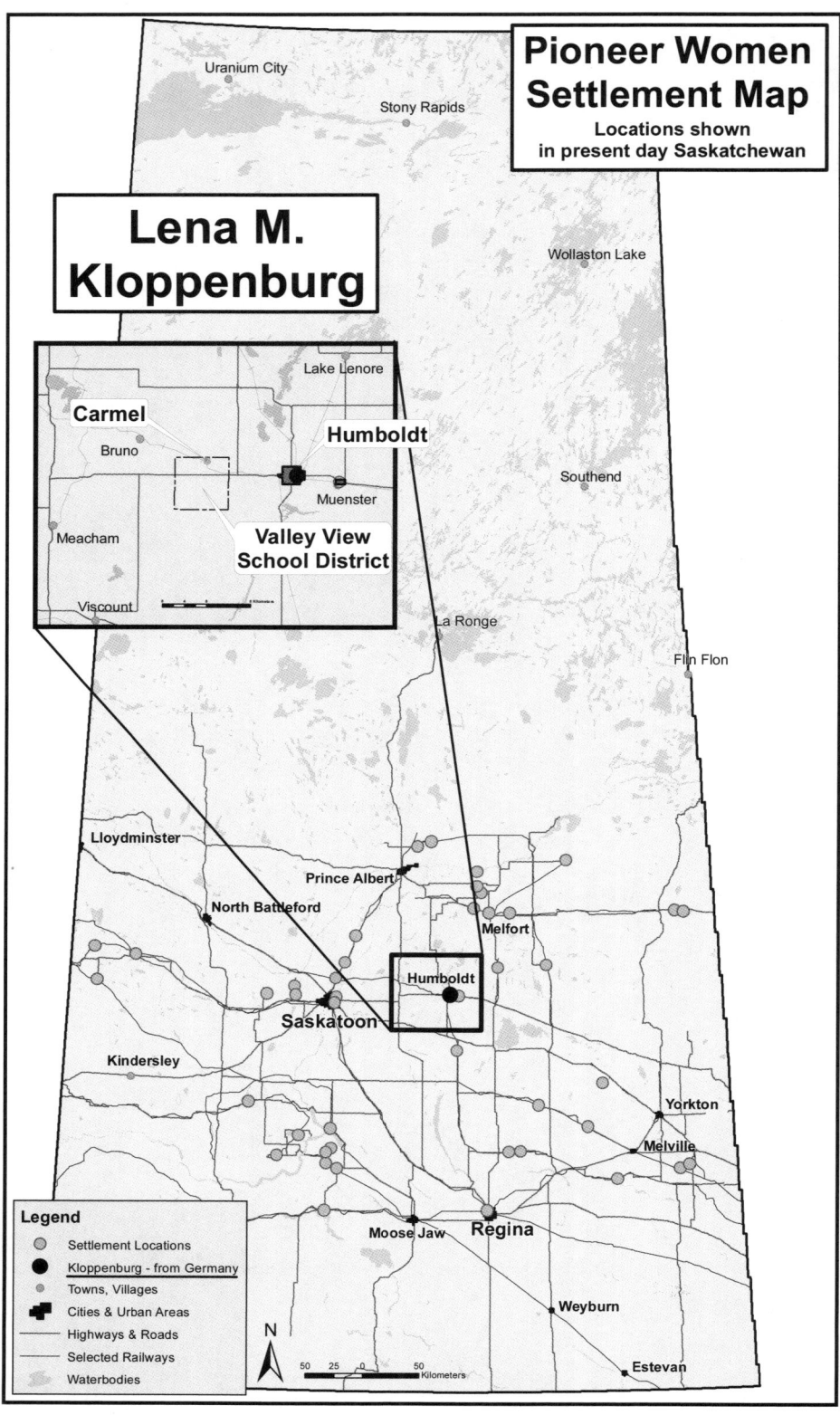

LENA M. KLOPPENBURG
(1915-1968)

Lena Kobelsky was born on May 31, 1915, in Carmel District, Saskatchewan, not far from the present city of Humboldt. She was the 13th of 15 children born to Michael and Regina Kobelsky, ethnic Germans who had immigrated to Canada in 1903 from southern Russia adjoining the Black Sea.

Her parents were descendants of German settlers who, during the reign of Catherine the Great, had migrated to Russia to improve agriculture there. They came to Canada because the Russian government no longer wanted German agricultural settlers and they, with many others, were no longer welcome in Russia. This was the same reason the Mennonites left Russia at about the same time.

Her father filed for a homestead near the site of the former Immaculate Conception Church. Lena took her formal education at Valley View School, a one-room, all-grades school located south of Carmel. She finished Grade 8 in 1929, the year of the great stock market crash that led to the Great Depression of the 1930s. Her career choices were thus severely limited. Attending high school would have meant paying tuition fees, unless a student's parents paid school taxes in the school district in which the student attended. Lena's family did not live in a district where a high school existed, so she did not get to high school. Her family was without financial resources to make education beyond Grade 8 possible. She could read and write well with a Grade 8 education.

Lena Kloppenburg

As a teenager, after Grade 8, she did housework for some of Humboldt's finer families. She observed their children attend university and do well in their lives. This greatly influenced her in later encouraging her own children to pursue a higher education. In her 20s, she took a hairdressing course. Lena was employed in that field until marriage. An explanation of her political sympathies was an event occurring between April 1944 and July 1944. In April 1944, Reverend T. C. Douglas formed a new government in Saskatchewan, defeating the Liberal premier W.J. Patterson. Shortly thereafter the provincial minimum wage inspector went to Humboldt and inspected the payroll record at the place where Lena was employed. The result was discovery of a wage underpayment of $500. That was an incredibly large amount of money in 1944 for a person earning less than $1.00 a day. The employer paid up and thereby indirectly financed Lena's wedding in July 1944.

She married Henry J. Kloppenburg, a German immigrant from Cloppenburg in Oldenburg, in what is now Lower Saxony. He had arrived in Canada from Germany in 1928. After marriage, they lived on a farm on the western boundary of Humboldt. Henry bought the farm from his father Anton after the Second World War for a modest price plus an annuity of 600 bushels of wheat. Anton did not trust governments to protect the value of the currency, given his experience of the inflation of the Weimar Republic in Germany.

After marriage, Lena was involved in the farm work in addition to housekeeping for the family. This included milking cows, managing a flock of chickens and attending to their slaughter, gardening and generally providing for a growing family. This was all done without the benefit of central heating, electricity (until 1951) or indoor plumbing (until 1957). In 1955, the advent of a deep freeze was a major event in her life. She was particularly involved in farm work during the harvest season.

Lena spoke a Low German dialect and learned Hochdeutsch[19] after marriage. Her eldest child Henry knew little English when he started school so for him, English was a second language. The family was very conscious of the history of 20th-century wars as her husband had had to report to Canadian police as an enemy alien during the Second World War. As one result, German cultural interests and language were not considered as important as assimilating the use of the English language in the local community.

Lena was a highly dedicated housekeeper for her family and was devoted to that job. She was thrifty, having survived the economic rigours of the Great Depression. She did not experience shopping beyond catalogue shopping, grocery shopping or the annual summer sale at Brusers' department store in Humboldt. The exception would have been a trip to Saskatoon to buy fabric for sewing. She was a fine seamstress with a treadle Singer sewing machine until she got an electric sewing machine in the 1960s. She made fruit preserves, jams, vegetables and sauerkraut. The family owned a maroon 1947 Studebaker car which was put on blocks for the winter. Once

---

[19] High German

the snow came, a sleigh and a caboose with horses was the main means of transportation. While she was accustomed to using a telephone when she worked in Humboldt, they did not have one on the farm until 1955.

Lena was most dedicated to the well-being of her children. She was a devoted mother of four to: Henry R. Kloppenburg (1945), Q.C., Rhodes Scholar and lawyer; Richard J. Kloppenburg (1949), retired; Dr. Lenore M. Kloppenburg (1951), obstetrician-gynecologist; and William J. Kloppenburg (1953), MBA. She was most concerned that her children did their homework and did well at it. She made sure that musical lessons were practised. She encouraged her children to read magazines and newspapers which she would pick up from more affluent families in Humboldt. Her own limited education did not equip her to help children with their homework.

Travel was but a limited part of her life. Between 1944 and 1965, it consisted of three trips to the Okanagan where Henry's brothers had been resettled after the onset of the Second World War from their previous location on the west coast. Then in 1965, she and Henry took a long-wanted trip to visit the place where he was born in Germany. This was a highlight of her last years.

She was active in Roman Catholic women's organizations in Humboldt and in the Humboldt Music Festival Association. She enjoyed cooking, having a large garden, and yes, having a flock of chickens and turkeys sufficient in number for the family's Thanksgiving and Christmas dinners and to share with others in her family. She was an accomplished seamstress, sewing for her daughter and herself. She was involved in the music festival in support of her children, of whom three were participants. She was also a member of the Catholic Women's League and an executive member of the Christian Mothers Society in the Catholic Parish of St. Augustine in Humboldt. She did other volunteer work in the Catholic Parish of St. Augustine from time to time.

Lena Kloppenburg died of cancer in 1968 at age 53. She underwent surgery to remove the cancer more than once but valiantly fought the ravages of that disease until November 9,

1968. Her husband Henry died in 2007 at age 95. They are both buried in the Roman Catholic cemetery at Humboldt.

By Henry Kloppenburg, son

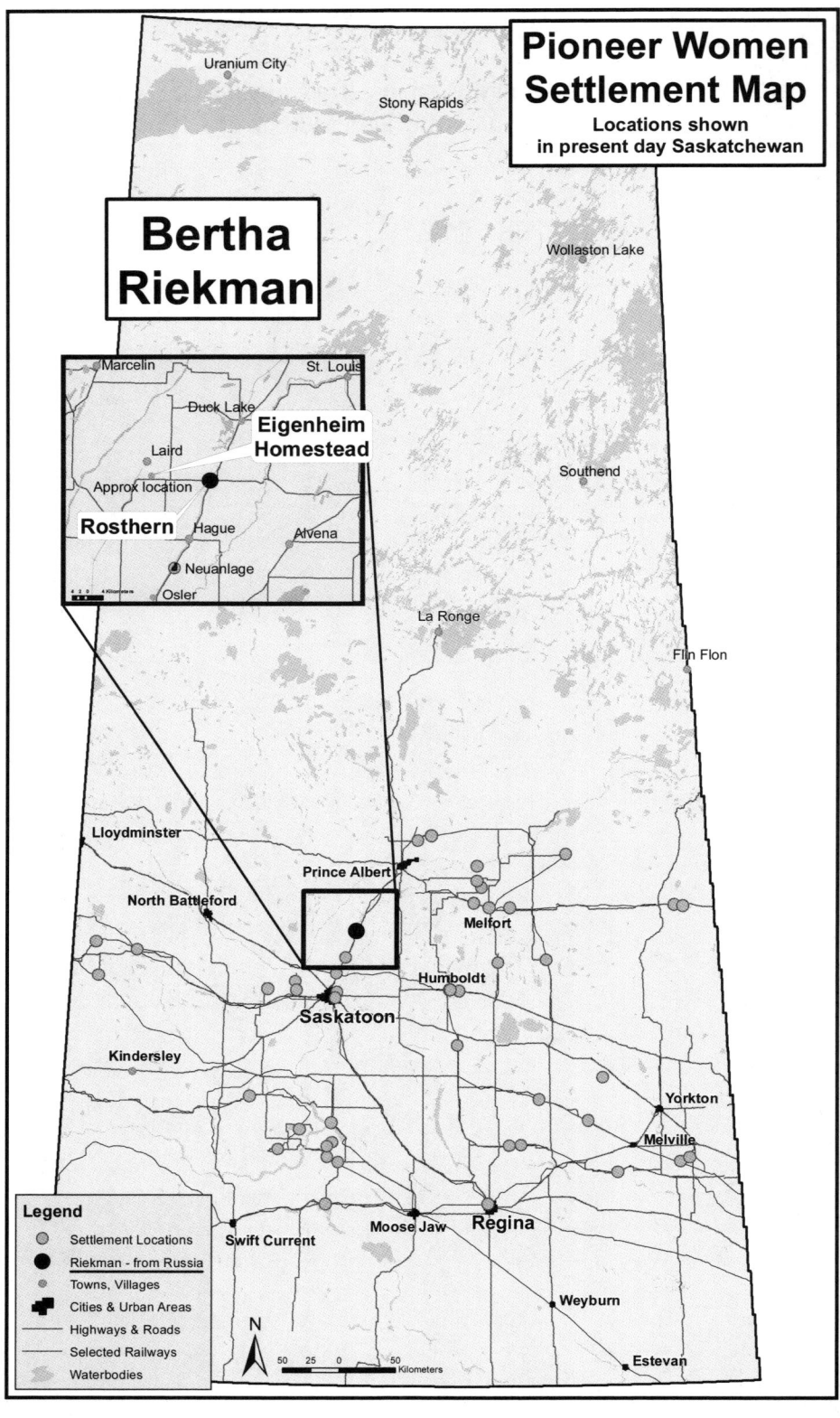

Bertha Riekman
(1915-2004)

Bertha was born on June 12, 1915, to Peter and Katharina Epp on her parents' homestead 10 miles west of Rosthern. Her grandparents, Heinrich and Margaretha Epp, immigrated to Saskatchewan from Fürstenland, Russia in 1891 when Katharina was eight years old.

When Bertha was a young teenager, her mother died. This was life-changing for Bertha, as she was then required to drop out of eighth grade and become the 'house person' for the large family. She had to cook and clean for her siblings – Otto, Wilmer, Benno, Elsie, Hilda and Frieda – and her father, which came by default because she was the oldest girl living at home. Her two older sisters, Marie and Martha, had married and left home by that time.

Family contacts led to Bertha taking a job in Ontario for several years during the Second World War. She worked as a cook for a wealthy family there and learned to make many gourmet dishes. She was required to learn more than the meat-and-potatoes dishes that she knew from home and worked with sauces, vegetables and meats that were not part of the farm life in Saskatchewan.

Bertha returned to Saskatchewan partway through the war and met Robert Riekman, a neighbour in the Eigenheim community, whose family lived about six miles west of Rosthern. Bertha and Robert were married on January 3, 1943, and moved to a grain and dairy farm three miles west of Rosthern.

Bertha and Robert Riekman with Caron and Carol

The dairy part of their farm always seemed to be needed to support the grain farming operation, with little left for the household. Farming was an occupation taken out of necessity and not choice, as there were few opportunities for them to pursue other careers.

Between 1946 and 1957, Bertha gave birth to seven children: Ruth (Don Neufeldt), Judy (Gary Ure), Katherine (David Hildebrandt), Erna (Tony Myers), Lloyd (Parvaneh Riekman), Carol (Felix Hoehn), and Caron (Ricky Lehman).

Bertha was mostly in charge of milking the cows, but raising the chickens allowed her to have money that she controlled for the extras that she desired to give her children and her family a better life. Every spring, a batch of baby chicks was purchased. By fall, the young hens were ready to lay eggs and the older hens were butchered for food. This meant the family no longer had only beef for meat. (Bertha's children found it hard to believe that their school friends envied them having steak and roast beef, while they actually desired their friends' salami and bologna sandwiches!)

Bertha was very particular about the gathering of the eggs. The eggs had to be gathered twice daily so the chickens would not begin to eat the eggs. Bertha kept the chickens in a pen and fed them chicken feed so that the eggs would be white – the colour with the highest demand – instead of tan or brown. Every day, in addition to washing the dishes, there were eggs to clean. This was a very specialized chore. The eggs that were already clean were never supposed to touch the water and the eggs that were minimally dirty were damp-wiped clean. Only the very dirty eggs were washed in water. The stained ones stayed home for the family to use.

The eggs always had to be placed in the cartons with the pointed side down. One day, Katherine asked her mother why this was done and was told it was due to the way the yolk settled in the egg. If the round side was down, the yolk settled on the bottom, making the egg difficult to be used for devilled eggs. Bertha made many dishes of eggs – scrambled with milk, scrambled with cream, fried, boiled, even boiled egg lasagne. The only type of egg that the family vetoed was devilled eggs because nobody liked them, so Katherine challenged her mother on this explanation of setting the eggs down specifically for devilled eggs. It was then that Bertha revealed that she was actually selling eggs to the local hotel. A lovely German lady there purchased a regular quantity of eggs from Bertha to make pickled eggs for the bar! Since Robert and Bertha were Mennonites and abstained from using alcohol, Bertha felt her children did not need to know about her biggest and most loyal customer!

Bertha was an amazing cook who had to abandon her gourmet cooking and resort to cooking more basic meat-and-potatoes meals to please the family at home. Bertha cooked the 'healthy way' before public awareness provided information on how to do so. She cooked low fat, lean meat meals with lots of vegetables and what she called the pure protein – eggs.

The money that Bertha received for the eggs was used for many extras. The children were all offered music lessons, but most of them did not make use of this offer. Bertha purchased her first freezer with the egg money, which allowed her to then plan meals ahead of time.

The extra money also allowed Bertha to purchase fabric for dresses. Each year, the girls received a new dress for Easter and a new dress for Christmas as well. Bertha was a great seamstress and made sure the style of the dresses was current with styles in the stores. Every year, their church had an auction sale to support the Mennonite Central Committee. Bertha purchased fabric and then sewed clothing – usually nightgowns – for the sale. The clothes she sewed were made to fit one of her girls but were more elaborate than the regular nightwear she usually made for her children. These nightgowns had a more difficult pattern and lace, too! Bertha then bid on the special nightgown and bought it back, as long as the bid was not too high. One year, Bertha deviated from making a nightgown and sewed a wardrobe for a doll. While her daughters longed for her to buy it back at auction, Bertha believed the wardrobe would bring more money for the mission than the nightgown would and it was sold to another bidder. Her daughters were pleased, however, to receive some other homemade doll clothes for Christmas.

Bertha and her mother-in-law Judith became good friends and the two of them altered and redesigned patterns, both believing that the clothes they sewed needed to look tailor-made, not homemade. Bertha and many other farm women of her generation were careful to recycle as much as possible, saving plastic bags and clothes that were in good enough condition to be used by someone else instead of being thrown away.

It was Bertha's desire that all of her children go to Bible camp at Pike Lake each summer. This required her to use egg money in addition to all of the quarters she had saved. Every time she had a quarter in her change purse, it was put into her tin can savings for camp.

Bertha was a very good listener and a woman of few words, so when she commented on the happenings in their family or community, her children listened. She encouraged her children to look at a person from that person's perspective instead of from someone looking in, and she lived that lifestyle. "We should not judge a person until we have walked in their shoes," she told her family.

Bertha lived life being a content woman. She never complained and if she desired anything, she never spoke about it until it was a goal she was working toward. She gave generously of her time and possessions, believing that we are rich in this country. She was thankful for all she had.

When their last children, Carol and Caron, were in grade 11, Robert finally realized his dream and purchased the Saskatchewan Government Insurance (SGI) business in Hague. Bertha no longer had her chickens but remained active in charity work with the Seniors Centre in Hague, helping where needed, including Meals on Wheels.

Bertha continued to support the Mennonite Central Committee in her retirement years by sewing many quilts and spending hours mending clothes that were donated to the Clothes Basket in order to make them saleable. Later, when her memory was fading, she coined the phrase, "You have to take it as it comes." This phrase is still used in that nursing home today.

Although she did not have a great singing voice, Bertha sang songs to her children that she felt were being lost – mostly the German choruses – while the children did chores like gardening with her.

Bertha was a Christian woman. Many times at the end of the day, the children went looking for their mother only to find her on her knees beside her bed.

Bertha died on December 31, 2004. She is buried in the Eigenheim Cemetery west of Rosthern.

By Katherine Hildebrandt, daughter

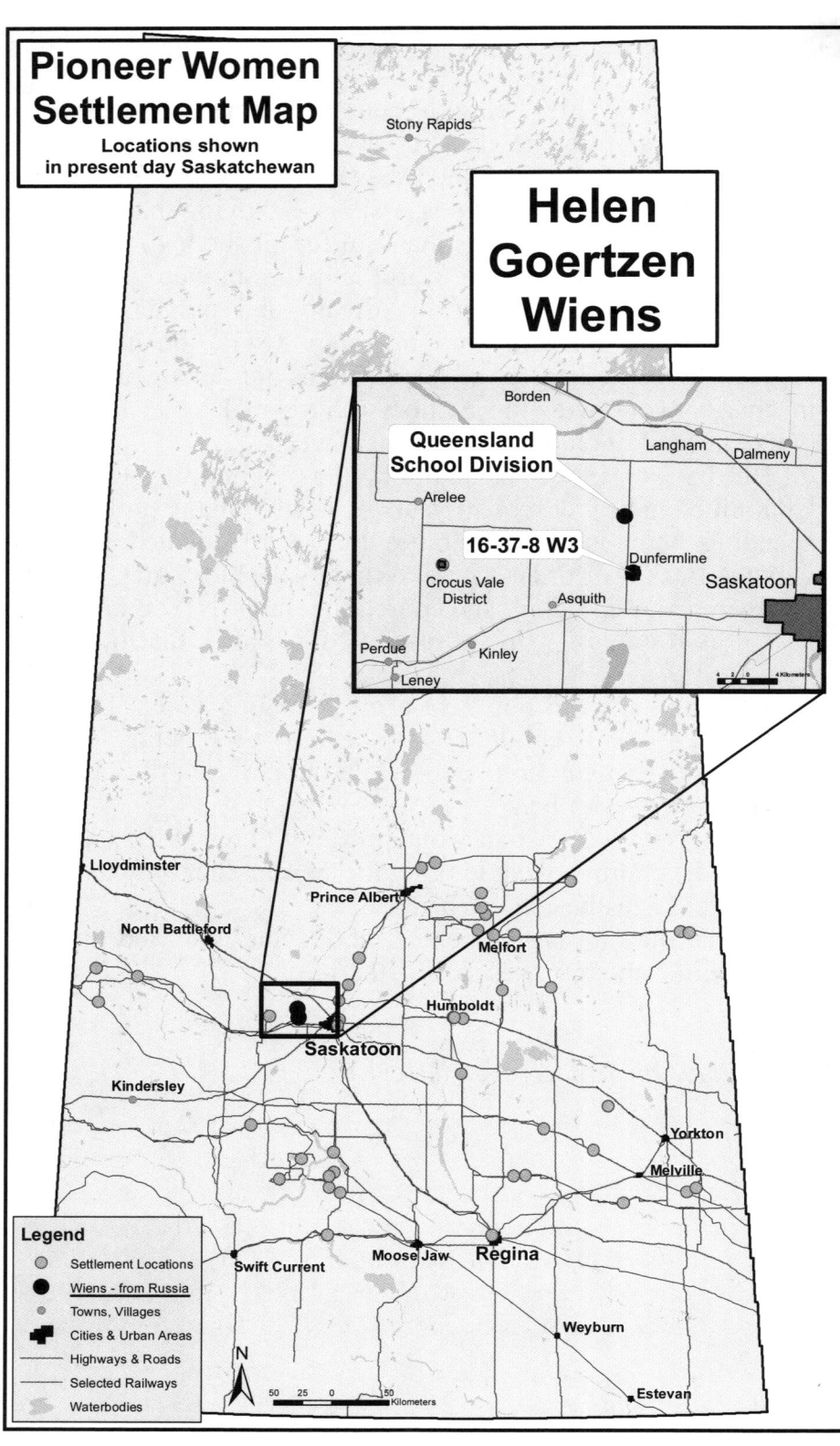

HELEN GOERTZEN WIENS
(1917-2000)

Helen was born in Russia on April 2, 1917. She came to Canada in September 1923 at age six with her parents Peter D. and Katherine Goertzen and siblings Katherina, Peter, David, Margaret, Henry, Mary and Annie. Helen was the third youngest child in her family. Hers was one of many Mennonite families that fled the political and social upheaval of Russia to seek a new life in Canada.

The Goertzen family purchased a quarter section of land in the Dunfermline area of Saskatchewan, 30 miles west of Saskatoon. It was light sandy soil with much bush and only 25 acres under cultivation. They cleared bush by hand and horsepower until they had cleared 75 acres upon which to grow grain and potatoes. Rows and rows of potatoes were planted, hoed and harvested by hand. Helen's mother suffered from rheumatoid arthritis, resulting in confinement to her chair. The three boys left home to find work elsewhere, so the job of growing and harvesting the potatoes fell to the girls.

Once the potatoes were dug, the girls made weekly trips to Saskatoon to sell the spuds door to door as well as to some grocery stores and cafes. Besides being loaded with the potatoes, the buggy (and later the Model T Ford) carried other garden produce, butter, cream, poultry and eggs. The revenue from these sales was a huge factor in not only sustaining the family through the Dirty Thirties but also in allowing Helen's father to pay off the debt owing on his farm. At a time when many Prairie farm families were facing bankruptcy, the

Helen and Cornelius Wiens and their children in 1952

Goertzen family survived, though humbly, mainly through the hard work of the daughters.

Helen's good character, combined with her red hair and slim figure, caught the eye of Cornelius Wiens, the son of a neighbouring farm family. After a brief courtship, the two were married on December 19, 1939, at the tiny rural church where both the Goertzen and Wiens families were members.

Soon after their marriage, Helen became pregnant with what would become the first of 10 children born in rapid succession. The eldest was nine years old when the tenth baby was born. It must have been for Helen that Loretta Lynn sang: "One of them a toddlin' and one is a crawlin' and one's on the way." By 1950, there were seven girls and three boys, including one set of twins. Seven years later, Helen became pregnant again but was unable to carry the pregnancy to full term. The baby boy lived only three days. It brought Helen much sorrow that she was too ill to see this baby or hold him in her arms.

Like most rural homemakers during the 1940s and 1950s, Helen had very few modern conveniences. Their first home was a wooden structure measuring 20 feet by 14 feet that Cornelius built by hand using only a hammer, nails and handsaw without the aid of a level or a square. This one room served as eating, sleeping and living quarters for Helen, Cornelius and their five little girls. During the summer of 1945, Cornelius built an addition to the house which added a main floor master bedroom and living room plus a second storey for children's bedrooms. The original room became the kitchen and dining area. In this modest home, Helen cooked, cleaned and cared for her family of 12.

For many years, a coal and wood stove was used for both cooking and heating. The wood and coal had to be hauled into the house and the ashes carried out. On chilly winter mornings, it was Helen who started the fire before heading out to the barn to help Cornelius with the milking. In spite of the heat of summer, she stoked the stove to prepare meals, to bake countless loaves of bread and to do the canning. Jars and jars of preserves lined the shelves in the cellar long before the cold weather set in. There were canned peas, beans, beet pickles, dills and saskatoon berry fruit, to name just a few. Electricity didn't come to the farm until the late 1950s, so Helen had no freezer to store food during those early years.

Cooking for a family of 12 was something Helen seemed to enjoy. Her homemade soups were delicious as well as nutritious. Supper was usually ready shortly after the children arrived home from school. The meals consisted mainly of meat – mostly pork – potatoes, and other vegetables. Sometimes stacks of thin pancakes awaited the children, or cottage cheese vereneki (perogy) or kielkah (a homemade noodle). On Fridays, as long as the cold weather lasted, the family ate fish, which Helen fried in a pan full of pork lard. The fish, frozen in crates of 100 pounds, were purchased from a business in the nearby town of Langham. On Saturdays, the menu was always homemade pork and beans, freshly baked zwieback (a Mennonite double-decker bun) and tea.

Roast chicken was a favourite meal of the family and was often served on Sundays. On Saturday night, two roosters met their doom at the chopping block. Then they were plucked with the help of hot water to loosen the feathers, singed over a capful of flammable liquid, and eviscerated. When the family returned home from church, there was a roaster full of the tasty fowl topped with wedges of potatoes and carrots ready for dinner.

Faspa, the Sunday supper served to relatives and friends who often dropped by unannounced, usually consisted of zwieback, jam, cheese, homemade cakes, cookies and coffee. This was the lighter meal served on Sunday evening. After a softball game with cousins or an afternoon of visiting with whoever dropped in, Helen provided a table laden with homemade buns, cakes, platz (a coffee cake made with a plum filling and sweet crumb topping) or cookies. As well, she always had a batch of peppermint cookies on hand since these were a must for Cornelius at the end of every meal.

Butchering hogs was done in late fall just as the cold weather set in. Two good-sized pigs were selected each year. Several families got together, taking turns hosting the event with each person specializing in at least one of the jobs involved. Helen was the person who would draw the pig – removing the entrails from the carcass that was suspended on a tripod. She also cleaned the intestines, which were then used as casings for the sausage.

Harvest was always a busy time of the year for the Prairie homemaker, who was responsible for providing meals for the threshing crew. Helen put in long days preparing food. First came a hearty breakfast, then a mid-morning lunch which was often delivered to the men out in the field. The noon-hour meal was huge – with meat, potatoes, vegetables and homemade bread as the staples. Pies were the dessert of choice. An afternoon lunch was packed up and taken out to the crew. Supper was another substantial meat-and-potatoes meal. Then there were all the dishes to do. There was no time for an afternoon nap at threshing time. Once farming technology advanced and Cornelius was able to purchase a combine, the family no longer needed the threshing crews but Helen still had plenty to do to help with the harvesting. She helped with the stooking, driving the grain truck and shovelling grain in the granary until the children were old enough to take over these chores. Of course, preparing meals was still necessary even after a day of working outside.

Helen loved gardening and never complained about all the work it entailed. It took years of hand cultivating and hoeing to get the plot of newly ploughed earth rid of thistles, wild rose bushes and other obnoxious weeds. Of course, some weeds thrived year after year so hoeing was a regular chore throughout the growing season. During dry spells, Helen hauled pails of water to the garden to keep the plants flourishing. Her garden was a source of pride, and friends and relatives who visited the farm were always taken for a tour through her huge garden.

Water had to be pumped at the outdoor well and hauled into the house for all cooking and cleaning. Water for doing dishes, bathing and laundry had to be heated on the stove. The dirty water had to be hauled out again after use. Helen, like mothers of her time, used cloth diapers for her babies. With one toddler barely out of diapers before the next baby arrived, Helen was continuously laundering diapers for 10 years, along with all the other household laundry. This involved hauling in the water, heating it on the stove, working the hand-operated washing machine, wringing out the clothes, piling loads of wet clothes on the table, then hauling out the used water and beginning the whole process again for the rinse cycle. Laundry was then hung on the outdoor clothesline to dry. In winter, Helen often draped wet tea towels over the backs of old chairs and set them outside to whiten in the sun. Many a cat felt the wrath of Helen's hand for squatting on the wet towels. After the wash was dry, the ironing process began because most clothes were cotton or linen and required ironing. Until Helen got a gas iron, and much later an electric one, she used flat irons[20], which had to be heated on the stove. The temperature had to be just right – too hot and the clothes were scorched, not hot enough and the wrinkles remained.

Helen had a special talent for sewing, knitting, darning and mending. She spent many hours at her treadle sewing machine fashioning clothes for her children and herself. Her creations

---

[20] Made of cast iron and heated to iron clothing

were done without the aid of a pattern. In one family portrait taken in 1952, all seven girls as well as Helen herself are wearing matching dresses she made. When Cornelius was in town doing business one day, wearing the overalls Helen had mended, the storeowner said to him, "Those are the neatest patches I've ever seen." Embroidery was another one of her passions. Family members all have sets of tea towels or pillowcases that she embroidered. She was also a talented quilter. A large quilting frame was a permanent fixture in the basement of her home. From her sewing projects, she saved the leftover pieces of cloth and from used clothing, she cut out the scraps of good fabric. She stitched these together to fashion beautiful quilts. Never were two the same. Each one was a work of art. In addition to all the quilts she made for personal use and donated for church projects, each of her 31 grandchildren received a piece of her handiwork in the form of a quilt.

Throughout her life, Helen struggled with various forms of ill health. She was a sickly child who at one point in early childhood was not expected to survive. Headaches were a constant menace. She often wound a cloth tightly over her forehead and carried on with her daily routine, which simply didn't allow for a day off in bed. She met every challenge with courage, dignity and sheer grit. She overcame bouts with ulcers, skin disease, diabetes, high blood pressure and heart attacks.

When Cornelius was stricken with Parkinson's disease, she vowed to "care for him until I drop." It was with much despair that she finally had to face the realization that she could no longer look after him and that he would have to move into the local seniors' home. Cornelius moved into the Langham Care Home in July 1999. Helen stayed in their house in town and went to visit as often as she could. One lonely year later, her own health failed and after some time spent in a Saskatoon hospital, she joined Cornelius in the care home. They were together there for a few short weeks before she succumbed to heart failure on August 27, 2000. Cornelius passed away on December 24, 2004. They are both buried in the Neuhoffnung Cemetery south of Langham at the site of the small country church where they were married.

Her children say that they could fill a book with all the memories of their mother. Here are just a few:

– She loved to play Chinese Checkers, always chose the black marbles and very seldom did anyone ever beat her.

– I remember walking past the old cook stove when Mom was frying meatballs for supper, grabbing one and tossing it from one hand to the other while sprinting up the stairs before popping the tasty morsel into my mouth.

– No one could pick saskatoon berries as fast or as clean as she did.

– When Dad's finger was nearly completely severed while sawing wood, she put on a splint and bandage which impressed even the doctor and nurses.

– She made me a coat of many colours long before Dolly Parton sang about hers.

– Driving with her could be rather scary especially when she was trying to keep the car on the road between ditches filled with water.

– I remember when the neighbour's dog came calling on our Fido and Mom sent him packing with a string of tin cans tied to his tail.

By Evangeline Lundgren, daughter

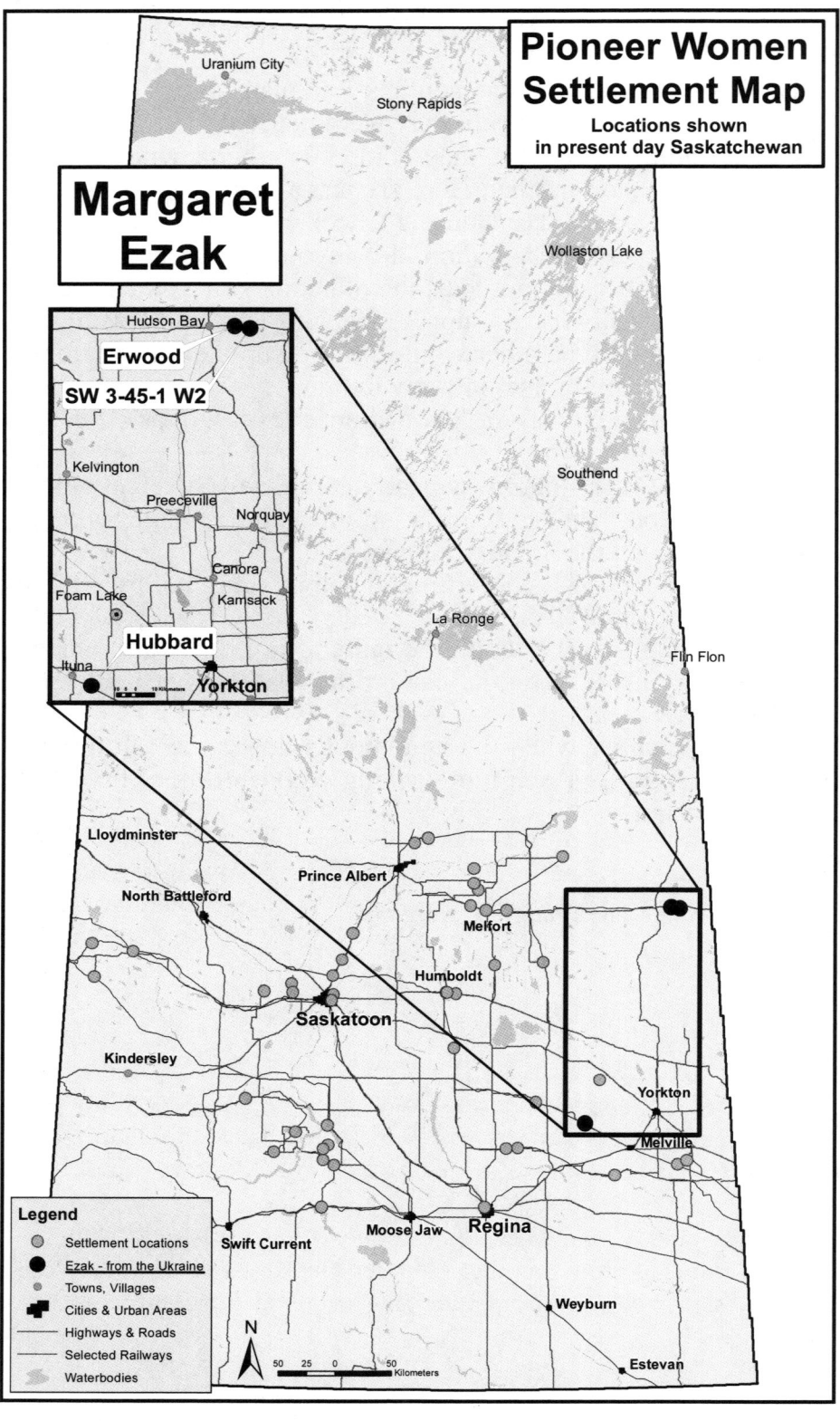

Margaret Ezak
(1923-2011)

Margaret was born in 1923 in Sarnia, Ukraine to Martha Nickunchuk and Julian Nikonetz. She was the second of four children born in the Ukraine who immigrated to Canada – Katie (1921), Margaret, Olga and John (1929). Four more siblings were born in Canada – Elsie (1933), Ann, Mary and Cecilia (1939).

Life in Ukraine was very difficult. They lived in a communal house with other families, some of whom were mean and envious of the children. There was a particular aunt who had no children of her own and often accused the children of mischief and got them into trouble. Margaret's parents wanted a better life for the family. In April 1929, Margaret's father left for Canada with the intent of bringing the family to Canada when he got established. Three years later, the rest of the family set sail across the ocean to join him in Hubbard, Saskatchewan.

Margaret often talked about the traumatic voyage crossing the ocean. It was a very scary adventure when she and her mother became seasick. Margaret felt like she was on her deathbed. They spent nine days at sea before arriving in Montreal, Quebec and travelled by rail to Saskatchewan. The family rented a house in Hubbard and Margaret and her siblings started school.

Margaret's academic experience was short-lived due in part to her age, the language barrier, the distance required for her travel to school (16.4 km) and her need for glasses. After

Margaret Ezak

two years, she dropped out of school and started working as a housekeeper/babysitter at a nearby farm.

During the Great Depression, the land surrounding Hubbard was infertile due to rust from crop disease, and it was very difficult to feed a family. Her older sister Katie had married and moved to the hamlet of Erwood. Katie encouraged the family to come to a better area where gardens grew and there was wildlife to hunt and better sustain a family. In 1937, the family moved to Erwood. The journey took nine days, travelling by horses and a hayrack. The trails were narrow and trees had to be cut down to allow the horses and rack to get through. The generosity and kindness of the people along the way, who shared their food and shelter with the family, was a special hospitality that Margaret never forgot.

In Erwood, they lived with Katie until they built a shack

for their own home. It took the family one year to clear 10 acres of land with an axe and hard labour. The children all helped with picking rocks and roots. The generosity of the neighbours was remarkable. Seed was shared to put in a garden and grow a small crop. The family preserved wild berries and meat to get them through the severe winters. Margaret's fondest memories of this time were the family get-togethers at their own and neighbours' homes, singing and sharing stories.

In 1938, Margaret married Mike Ezak, who had purchased a homestead three years earlier in the Smoking Tent district five miles east of Erwood. The homestead was offered by the government for $10. Mike cleared the land and built a log house into which they moved at the time of their marriage. They slowly cleared more of the land by hand and built up a mixed farming operation over the years with cereal crops, a garden, pigs, chickens, cattle, horses and sheep. "Little by little, we had more food, more seed, more animals and more land. We always had lots to eat," Margaret reflected. "On most Sundays, ice cream was made with fresh cream, ice from an ice house and the manual cranking of an ice cream maker. The children enjoyed taking turns cranking the machine. There was much laughter, singing and just having a great time." The butter churn was another machine that brought great joy to Margaret and Mike's four children: Natalie (1940), Dorothy (Doris), Sally and Peter (1945).

In addition to all of the work required to survive and raise a family on the farm, Margaret helped by supplementing the family income selling cheese, cream, eggs, produce from her garden and other goods such as yarn that she spun and knitted into mittens and socks.

It is hard to comprehend the volume and degree of physical work required to maintain a household on a homestead in northeastern Saskatchewan in the mid 1900s. There was no running water. The well was in the middle of the yard and not very reliable in the winter. Central heat was supplied by a wood stove in the kitchen. Farm labourers were hired seasonally and needed to be fed. Meal preparation was a huge task at threshing time and was completed with fresh, all-natural farm ingredients. There were no shortcuts to stitch together the periods of joy with family and fellowship with neighbours.

Margaret and Mike farmed until 1972, when they retired to Saskatoon. Margaret found the transition to be very difficult as she left behind many great friends and the wide open spaces. She soon learned the local bus route and busied herself by babysitting and house cleaning. She continued to grow a huge vegetable and flower garden. Fall was a very busy time of cleaning up her garden and making her own sauerkraut and preserves.

Margaret had a strong work ethic and was determined to be independent and self-supporting. Her most redeeming characteristic was her genuine kindness and care for those around her. She always took care of others before herself. She loved gatherings with family and friends. She was frugal with her own needs but very extravagant with her family. Margaret never stopped learning and pursuing all life challenges that came before her. She was a very proud mother, grandmother and great grandmother. Her family and heritage were very important to her and she was honoured to be a participant in the Egg Money project recognizing pioneer women of Saskatchewan.

Margaret resided in Saskatoon at Parkridge Centre until her death on November 22, 2011. She is buried in Woodlawn Cemetery in Saskatoon.

By Dorothy (Doris) Yuel, daughter

ACKNOWLEDGEMENTS

The German Days Book Publishing Committee –
Barbara Hoggard-Lulay (Chair), Brigitte Boldt-Leppin,
Rosa Gebhardt and Barbara Stehwien – would like to thank
the families of the 24 remarkable women portrayed
in this book for their much appreciated contributions
to the 'Egg Money' project.